Chairs of Discipline

Steven J Parker

2010

This book is dedicated to the students, faculty, and my family who inspired me through the tough times

A special thanks to the coeditors:

Amy Parker-Fiebelkorn
John Parker
Lynn Lindau

Table of Contents

Table of Contents (Continued)

Prologue
February 1997

Caledra Union High School, Caledra, WI

My heart pounded as I waited in one of two chairs outside the closed door of the assistant high school principal's office.

"I am sitting in the *chairs of discipline*," I muttered. "These chairs are for students who are in trouble-the druggies, the truants, the bullies, the stealers, the fighters, the foul mouth artists, the failures, and the violators of all other aspects of the student code," I thought to myself. "Why was I summoned here this time?" The pessimist side of me had a hunch that principals don't schedule conferences with a teacher unless the latter, in this case me, did something wrong. It wasn't the first time I was convened here, and it likely wasn't going to be the last.

I momentarily recollected minding my own business monitoring the hall in the passing minutes between seventh and eighth period earlier that day when the assistant principal, Mr. Jonas, popped up from out of nowhere.

"Steve, I need to see you in my office after school today," he bristled before disappearing out of view amidst the sea of student bodies. The mandate stabbed me in the heart. The edgy tone of his voice bespoke anger and frustration. I frantically brainstormed what might have angered the administrative gods this time. Even little Chelsea, an incoming eighth hour student, couldn't interrupt my trance of fear with her daily annoying greeting, "*So*, what are we doing today?"

All I could think about was to what degree I was toast. School administration did not need to have a reason to fire a non-tenured new teacher like me. Is it possible Mr. Jonas knew about the most recent horrors I experienced in the classroom as a new teacher? If so, I'll lie to him and say it's all under control and that I am slowly progress-"... "Um, Mr. Parker, Mr. Jonas will see you now," the secretary cut in.

I bit my lower lip and let out one last deep, nervous-stricken breath before mustering the courage to stand up. My jitteriness turned to trepidation as I slowly rounded the corner into his small office.

"Have a seat," he gestured. His eyes were locked in on mine. At 6'3", he had an imposing figure for a boss. Everything about his attire bespoke business, from the power tie to his scholarly spectacles. The door swung shut, leaving nowhere for me to hide in his small cubicle. I braced myself for what was to come as he painstakingly thought of the words to say.

"Steve, I've been talking to many of your students. They simply aren't getting it - your lessons, that is. I am beginning to wonder if you are focusing too much on discipline and not enough on education ... we have to make it through the year,

Steve … by the way, I want names of the students who are stealing the lenses off the microscopes."

Mortified, I gasped. "He *does* know about the vandalism!"

With that, the meeting was over. Dazed by the daunting ultimatums, I staggered out of his office with my tail between my legs. "God help me. How *am* I going to survive the last four months of the school year?"

Aftershock of Mr. Jonas' Summons

I retreated from Mr. Jonas' office mortified, confused, and agitated. He knows everything. What did he mean by, "I've been talking to many of your students?" What was I supposed to make of that? I replayed that statement over and over in my mind. Who has been talking? How often and where have they been doing it? Exactly what have they been talking about? That aforementioned revelation blindsided me. At this point in time, a colleague could have said, "Hi," to me in the hallway and I wouldn't have noticed.

I suddenly had the urge to know who was digging up dirt on me! Mr. Jonas rarely is seen down our science hallway, so he couldn't possibly be eavesdropping on my classes, unless he could hear the clamor of my classes all the way down the hall. Have my students been volunteering information to him or has he been pressuring them to talk? Who are the moles, ratting on my tribulations? Since my classroom has become a hot zone for disciplinary issues, does he now feel an obligation to intervene?

Supposedly, rumor has it that the new teacher is going through hell. Everyone seems to be talking about me behind my back. Why should the gossipers care how bad they vilify and mock me? I won't be around next year to look them square in their ashamed eyes. They knew I was only under a one-year contract, filling in for Mr. Blathe, who was in Australia for a sabbatical.

If a confidant approached you and said your coworkers were gossiping about you behind your back, you also would yearn to know whom, why, and what about. You cannot exonerate yourself from the partial lies you never hear. That is what bothered me about my conference with Mr. Jonas. "I've been talking to many of your students." What the hell was that supposed to mean? Since when do you invest faith in testimonials from guilt-ridden, lazy adolescents who are taking advantage of me? "They aren't getting it," referencing the curriculum. You don't say! Gee, if those little rats spent half as much energy paying attention to the lesson as they did talking in class, they would be passing with flying colors!

I began to wonder if the focus of Mr. Jonas' surveillance was on the troublemaking students or on me. If it was the latter, maybe he had assigned scouts to report back to him. Fielding phone calls from angry parents had to be the ultimate reason he summoned me into his office in the first place. The concerned parents probably felt they were doing the field of education a service by attempting to weed what they perceived to be "bad" teachers like me out of the system. Maybe parents got irate come report card time when their 'prodigal child' wasn't making the grade, then called the administrator to blame me. Even if their children's F was well deserved, somebody had to be the scapegoat, so why not make it the new teacher that "didn't know any better"? It would not surprise me if Samantha's Rippart's anal, angry mom prompted this meeting.

Samantha always sat in my classroom smitten with disdain. She stared at her desk most of the class period and doodled. Her forearm got a daily workout, keeping her head propped up during class. She was visibly irritated as a "victim" of the classroom noise and unruliness. As time went on, she became a sounding board to her mom.

One time, Samantha Rippart approached me in class during work time, worried over how to do an open-ended project. She was the type of student who needed structure. She needed directions to follow every step of the way, with the i's dotted and the t's crossed. She panicked upon hearing my answer inviting her to be creative. She begged me to change her rubric and treat her differently than her peers. She didn't want me to diversify her way of learning. She sought her comfort zone by getting me to allow her to complete the project the only way she knew how, and that was by following a detailed instruction manual, sans imagination. Now perturbed, I dryly told her to "Wing it." The next day, Mrs. Rippart gave Mr. Jonas an earful to ensure the complaint boomeranged back to me.

A self-anointed failure, I was jaded and humiliated. I could only spend my energy once. Was I going to spend it on teaching or disciplining? No teacher can have the former without the latter. Focusing less on discipline would not cause the disruptive behavior to go away. What choice did I have but to raise my voice and teach over the side bar conversations to reach the few who cared? I couldn't send the talkers to the back lab area of the room because there already had been too much vandalism to the microscopes and lab drawers during supervised labs.

Had it not been for the threat of vandalism, I would have let the talkative students camp out in the back of the room, thereby allowing the serious learners to stay up front with me. I could then focus on the latter without having to lecture over the disruptive ones as they exercised their right to fail. Come to think of it, my disruptive students are destined to become my colleagues' problem next year. If my assigned mentors saw their role as a formality without taking time to check up on me, then they will be the ones paying the price next year when they are assigned all of the additional students who failed my classes this year. I don't blame my mentors; rather, the pseudo mentoring programs are to blame most public schools had in place in the mid-late 1990s. It seemed a majority of the designated mentors lacked training. Schools offered no specified guidelines and timelines for new teacher – mentor conferences, let alone time for the new teacher to meet with the mentor(s) during contractual hours.

Up to this point in time, I waged war against the rebellious students through disciplinary action. They outnumbered me with protection in numbers. They couldn't ALL be wrong, which is why Mr. Jonas advised me in a military sense to stand down on the class time wasted on disciplinary assault. I compromised student learning for discipline and I should have known better with a collegiate degree.

Some students lost respect for me the second I called them by their requested nickname the first day of school. Others like Marge Beyland stopped acknowledging me when I couldn't remember her name in the hallway one morning. Others lost respect for me over the inequality of how I only disciplined the boys for talking. Whatever reason they created, I should have seen it coming. Over ninety percent of the student feedback essays at the end of my student teaching practicum the previous fall read I was "too nice of a teacher." I should have known students don't respect nice teachers because nice teachers don't have classroom control.

I found myself at the crossroads of my profession less than a year logged in. The only student who seemed to care about me at this juncture was Olivia Baker. To my dismay, her attention was crush-driven. Her untimely visits to our recessed office area embarrassed me in front of my colleagues. She periodically solicited chummy notes and surprised me with hand-made, personalized holiday cards, which were undoubtedly a generation ahead of its time by today's Stampin' standards. One day Olivia walked right past the science secretary in the entryway on up to my desk and began making small talk. Busy filing papers, I never turned to acknowledge her. She stood next to me seemingly forever before she finally got the hint and said, "Well, I hope you have a better day, Steve." Steve?!? Since when were you ever permitted to address me by my first name? I turned to correct her, but she was gone.

Regardless, Mr. Jonas was right. I needed to make it through the school year. I was taking on too many problems alone, yet no one seemed able to help me. I became desensitized to condolences and words of encouragement. There was not much I could do because the window of opportunity I had to gain my students' respect was long past. My dream profession had become a nightmare. Was I ever going to wake up to a better tomorrow?

Scars
Summer of 2007

Life is good. I couldn't think of a better place to be than at the lake home of our dearest friends, with a refreshing ice-cold gin and tonic in hand on a sweltering, hot summer day. Our hosts then invited us on a pontoon ride around their lake, so I made a pit stop in their bathroom. Before returning to the warm hospitality of our long-lost friends, I made a passing glance at the mirror. I stopped dead in my tracks. I back peddled a step and gazed in the mirror again.

"This can't be happening. No, not again. NOT AGAIN!" Three pronounced patches of white flakes surfaced on my face. My facial dandruff was back, damn it. How long had I been parading around today with this embarrassing exfoliation?

Almost ten years had passed since the embarrassing dandruff first appeared on my face. The white flakes first broke out mid-year during my tenure as a first year teacher at Caledra Union High School. To this day I believe the visible facial dandruff is stress-induced. The horrors I experienced teaching that first year activated a dormant gene that coded for it, and now I am plagued with reoccurring facial dandruff whenever stresses get the best of me. Not being a dermatologist, I thought it initially was a unique form of skin rash. I had never heard of dandruff on the face. Facial dandruff is very noticeable-just ask my wife every time she reaches over to scrape it off.

Today, I was once again cursed with white flakes of skin that covered a red backdrop of new, tender skin. If I scraped off the dandruff, the underlying red skin would become a fragmented white mosaic tomorrow as a new layer of dandruff. For years, I battled the exfoliation with a prescribed steroid-based ointment, which caused the treated areas to glisten like lip gloss all day long.

If I couldn't keep the stress-induced dandruff off of my face during the most relaxing time of summer, then it was time for me to grow a goatee. If I couldn't get rid of it, then I had to somehow cover it up. With my light brown hair, a five o'clock shadow wasn't going to get the job done. Operation cover-up needed a grown out manly goatee. The question was would I look good with one? I had never grown one out before that I thought looked halfway decent. I convinced myself that it was better to sport an ugly, scraggly goatee than it was to announce to the world I had blistering white dandruff sloughing off of my face. I would spare everyone in the future the awkwardness of gathering the courage to inform me, Mr. Poor Hygiene, I had 'white crud' on my face.

To this day, I suffer from periodic patches of dandruff on my cheeks, nose, neck, and in my sideburns and eyebrows. The condition is known as Sebhorric dermatitis.   Soon after I treat the affected areas, facial dander pops up in other areas. It reminds me of Elmer Fudd's pathetic attempt to flush Bugs Bunny out of the rabbit hole in classic Looney Tunes episodes. He repeatedly aimed the barrel of his shotgun down one rabbit hole, while

Bugs popped out of the next one over, carrot in hand, asking, "What's up, Doc?" In battling my Seborrhic dermatitis, I am Elmer Fudd. Bugs Bunny is the dandruff, here to stay, laughing at me. At least most people who have dandruff of the scalp can conceal the majority of the flakes with their hair.

I realized that during one of the most relaxing junctures of summer I could not escape the scars of stress that dated back to my first year of teaching. I looked at my cheeks and thought to myself, "how many skin layers have I prematurely lost over the last ten years? A thousand? Two thousand? Four thousand? Hey, it's plausible considering that for many years I scraped off a layer of skin dander *every day*. Multiply that figure by 365 days in a year and we have ourselves one hell of a number. I refuse to think about the possibilities of long-term scars.

For the time being, I must be thick skinned. I had to be thick skinned to survive my first year of teaching. I held a lot in that year. My parents could tell that something was wrong because they knew me. They felt bad for me every time I fell silent when queried about how my job was going. The uncomfortable silence I gave in answer to that repeated question was my way of sparing them and myself the horrors of teaching I was not ready to relive. I continuously questioned how much longer could I take on those hardships.

I eventually arrived at a professional crossroads. I had to question if the teaching profession was right for me. That was hard to do because I wasn't ready to throw thousands of dollars invested in collegiate training down the drain. It would be harder yet for me to walk away from the profession without feeling guilty for being a quitter.

First Year Teachers

Be careful, Steve. The harder new teachers like you strive to succeed, the more susceptible you are to burn out. You soon will discover there is nowhere near enough time to do everything you want to do. You will find yourself teaching lessons off of curriculum you wrote the morning of. You fortunately won't have time to envy your veteran colleagues for being amazingly confident and efficient at what they do.

The general public is clueless over the astonishing amount of time caring new teachers like you will spend developing curriculum. Sadly, even if they were enlightened over the one hundred plus hour workweeks you will log each of your first few years, many wouldn't care. Some members of the general populace are guaranteed to even be cynical over all the extra hours you will donate to the school. Writing tests, worksheets, rubrics handouts, lab manuals, and quizzes for the first time are all daunting, time-consuming tasks.

As a college graduate, you are at least four years removed from the last time you took a meaningful course in your major that would help you teach at the secondary level. For example, there is no way college physical chemistry is going to help you teach physical science, even though it maybe the only required course keeping you from earning the chemistry minor, needed to become licensed to teach chemistry.

Everything is harder the first year. All veteran teachers have to do is click the computer mouse to retrieve, copy, and paste last years' lessons onto the current year lesson planner program. As a new teacher, you won't have that luxury. Some don't even receive help from their veteran colleagues because they are too possessive to share their lessons. Hopefully, veteran teachers you work with will wisely facilitate a balanced system of a shared workload by encouraging you to write your share of lesson plans to complement the ones you burrow from them. This will enable you to cultivate your own pedagogic style without having to reinvent the wheel.

As the new teacher, chances are you will be naïve at gauging how long traditional lessons are supposed to take due to miscalculated time estimation for the activities therein. Pay attention, Steve. Your colleagues will ask you to pen the March lesson plans for your science department on comparative anatomy. Regardless of this advice, you will stubbornly plan the fetal pig dissection to take three days before your colleagues musingly correct you with notice the feature dissection would span at least two weeks.

Discipline will be your most onerous task. There won't be much of an age difference between you and your upper class students. Some seniors date alumni the same age as you, and therefore will have difficulty discerning you as a professional from a contemporary.

You won't know the names of your new students the first week of school, which will put you at a huge disadvantage in comparison to your veteran colleagues. Many veteran teachers know students by name on day one as either returning students, or as younger siblings of former students. Not knowing students' names will make it difficult for you to promptly address call outs and disruptive behavior on a personal level, especially if they are simultaneously talking out of turn. In those instances, you will have a split second to effectively react verbally or nonverbally. If the disruption to the lesson warrants a verbal warning, don't generically warn the transgressing students because they will always have an advantage of remaining ambiguous in misconduct.

Students will test you to see what they can get away with. They know the second there is inconsistency in the disciplinary enforcement of your classroom policies a can of worms is opened up for chaos and fun. Class will then become a game, where the students pit themselves against you, the teacher, at the expense of education.

Youthfulness furnishes most first year teachers with enough energy to survive. Even though you trained your body to function on little sleep in college, you will soon learn teaching will enervate you like nothing you have experienced before. It's a good thing you are not married because if you were, your spouse would accuse you of being married to your profession. That is the price fledgling teachers pay when there seemingly isn't enough time in the day to perform the job to the best of their ability. In your case, however, it will take a prayer to survive your first year on the job because you won't heed these warnings. The

20

frustrations you will experience over the shortage of time needed to fulfill your job expectations will become the least of your concerns.

Welcome to the new school year, Steve. Don't let your mistakes bleed because you soon will be swimming into shark-infested waters. Your students will eat you alive for the next nine and a half months until school lets out in mid-June. Prepare to tread water and bleed out your mistakes through sweat and tears. If you survive until the final bell of the school year, what's left of you will get reprieve then.

Sunrise Butterflies

Exhale Steve; it all comes down to this. Four and a half years of classes, lecture halls, final exams, field experiences, assigned readings, and dreams of great things to come. The best things in life are supposed to come to those who delay the gratification of a decent wage after four and a half years of college. I stepped out of my rusted teal Chevy Tahoe and sallied forth into the building called Caledra Union High School. Today the front entrance was unlocked, unlike yesterday, when I learned that even teachers did not have building access during weekends. In a few more steps, I was about to put my hard-earned collegiate degree into motion.

A couple of early bird students had beaten me to school and were trying out their new locker combs. My first fleeting thought was they simply couldn't wait for the summer doldrums to end to reconnect with their friends. On second thought, they could have been early drop offs of parents en route to work. Then again, they could be the unfortunate progeny of fellow teachers who had no choice in the matter but to arrive early. Regardless, I just hoped they weren't the type of student who prefers only to socialize with adults because they don't relate to their peers. I encountered a couple of students like that while student teaching in McAllen, Texas. They predictably arrived at school early on a daily basis with the longing to socialize with teachers. In a perfect world, teachers should not shun the social needs of those children. I learned from my practicum experience, however, that it pays dividends to lock the classroom door to protect the precious waning minutes of preparatory time leading up to the start of each day of school. Surely, the office personnel were keeping tabs on the two vagabond teens through surveillance cameras. With Caledra being a satellite suburb of Milwaukee, this sprawling building was not the studio where the innocent, small town school experience was filmed in the TV sitcom, *Saved by the Bell*.

My attention immediately shifted to my squeaky shoes on the shiny hallway floor. The recently waxed floor is the only red carpet treatment students and staff will get this year so I had better appreciate it while it lasts. Thank you, fellow taxpayers. And thank you, fellow custodians for exhausting your last ounce of energy to meet unrealistic late summer deadlines hurled at you. You deserve a much-needed rest.

I turned down the corridor leading towards my home base, the science department. Upon entering the office area, a secretary greeted me.

"Hello, I am Marcy, the science department secretary," she said.

It didn't take long for that uncommon name to fade from my short-term memory. I never was good with names, yet here I found myself a teacher expected to be good with name retention. Deep down, I grew up assuming all teachers *had* to go through name recollection training because surely, they all couldn't be gifted in that regard.

After exchanging some pleasantries, she wanted to know more about me. Being a new face in the department, I shared a superficial profile of myself to appease her curiosity. I then realized everyone today was going to be curious, so I had better get used to it. I needed to work on successful introductions because first impressions meant everything. And somewhere along the way, I will have to sell my services to my colleagues. You know the routine- convince them I belong and that I am one of them, notwithstanding the fact I am green behind the ears and fresh out of college.

She ushered me back to the office area. The place was an absolute mess. All of the cubicles were in disarray, with half of them under plastic tarp paper. Dust and debris canvassed everything.

"I apologize for the mess," she quipped. "As you can tell, the wing of this building is brand new and they (the custodians) still have yet to make their way back here to clean this up. Surely you understand. I figure it must have been the utmost importance for them to make sure the classrooms, hallways, and bathrooms were ready to go first. I believe your work desk is this dark gray one, if you can access it."

I pondered the irony over having a private work area, but felt homeless because I couldn't access it yet. It didn't matter because all I brought with me was my briefcase with the original copy of my 'House Rulz,' which that I was going to lay on the students today.

I couldn't wait to show my students who the boss was. They soon will know their place, their responsibilities, and their expectations. And they will know me. Just remember, Steve. Don't smile until after Christmas. My college education professors couldn't be wrong with that sagacious advice. I was so ready for my first period class that my enthusiasm flirted with boredom.

Fast-forward the clock. Ten minutes remained until the start of the first period. Over two thousand students now packed the hallways. En route to my classroom, I encountered an upper classmen, donning a baseball cap, standing amidst his posse of friends.

"Hey!" I snapped. "Caps aren't to be worn in school!" I glared down at him until he slowly removed it from his head. "Thank you," I said as I walked on by. Hah! How about that? I just asserted my authority to some punk who thought school policy didn't apply to him. It was later brought to my attention that although the wearing of hats violated student code at Caledra Union, no staff member enforced it before first period and after eighth period. With that said, I am certain that the moment I left, the reprimanded student put his hat back on. He knew the system. Little did I know that I would soon be in for a rude awakening. Today I was about to experience the calm before the storm.

Five classes awaited me on my schedule: four biology classes and a physical science. Without past yearbooks to consult, my class lists remained a conglomerate of names without faces.

This was the moment of truth. I had already signed off on my $600 union dues, so there was no turning back now.

I stood behind the front podium and took a deep breath. The warning bell for first period sounded, signaling the end of my nervous solitude. In a few minutes, I was about to lay down the 'House Rulz.'

The portioned pile of 'House Rulz' felt warm in my palm. Procrastination caused me to run the blue font copies off from an old mimeograph machine in our backroom, because there was too long of a wait at the big district copy machine. The first day of school is not the time to wait in line. Actually, there never is a line at the district copy machine, because teachers are not allowed to run off their own copies here. In a big district like this, a district secretary does it for you, as long as she has your hardcopy requisition three days in advance. Welcome to the teaching profession, Mr. Parker. If you are going to survive, you are going to have to plan not just ahead, but way ahead. Forget about the last minute ideas, even if they are the best. Getting to know the district secretary was paramount, if I stood a chance of ever getting copies without the three-day wait.

Getting on good terms with the janitors was my second survival goal, which I had yet to do. I was never going to win over their favor if I was nothing but needy. My third and most important survival rule was to start the year out tough. Don't smile. I was not here to be the students' friend.

'House Rulz'

I must have been day dreaming the day our education professor warned us about having too many classroom rules, that is *if* my college professors ever warned us not to have too many classroom rules. I more than made up for the teachers who were short winded on the first day. I should have pruned my classroom rules down to only the ones that were enforceable. Less is more. Think of the last time you painstakingly sat through an hour-long sermon where the message got so muddled with extraneous detail that the focus of the message was lost. In hindsight, that describes the monotonous monologue of my 'House Rulz.'

There were thirty 'House Rulz' in all. I was proud to have scripted each and every one of them. Can you believe 'No whining allowed' was one of them? How would I ever enforce that? Answering out of turn was a pet peeve of mine, and by golly, they needed to know that as rule number nineteen. Since I didn't want students to get up out of their desk to sharpen their pencil while I was lecturing, I decided to make that rule number twenty-three. Rule number twenty-four was 'No answers accepted on submitted work in red ink'. I surely didn't want students to crowd the doorway at the end of class, so it was imperative I barked that rule out to them as rule number twenty-eight. It didn't take long for each petty rule to add up. I had fun brainstorming the list. I thought I was so prepared. Communication is the key to being a successful educator, and my goal that day was to communicate my rules and expectations with my "comrades". They needed to hear all my pet peeves, so they could dutifully avoid them.

I still don't know what the hell I was thinking by having thirty rules and calling them the 'House Rulz'. To make matters worse, I unintentionally impersonated Ben Stein from the movie *Ferris Buellers' Day Off* in how I monotonously read the 'Rulz' to my students. Was I subconsciously trying to fit in with the gangs in this satellite suburb school of Milwaukee? Were there gangs even here? I recall successfully implementing a rapper lesson in college in front of my evaluating peers. It was one of the simulated lessons we had to teach on campus, and it was a hit. I learned that day how valuable incorporating rap into lessons was in helping students relate to the curriculum. I had the sudden ambition to develop curriculum utilizing rap songs laden with biological terms, which was a genre of music I knew little about.

Nonetheless, I didn't pontificate the 'Rulz' to my students the first day via rap song. The title of my 'Rulz' handout simply had rapper undertones. I naively assumed the 'Rulz' would be a hit and I would be a hit, while going on cruise control for the rest of the year.

The 'House Rulz' initiated a series of mistakes that were the death knell of my professional dreams in Caledra. Had I saved and published them in this book, I guarantee you it would have elicited an "Oh my God" knee jerk reaction from fellow educators in disbelief. Heck, I could envision them anointing me with a scarlet letter of the educational world, for my embarrassing first day of sins.

I did not question my teaching ability prior to my year at Caledra Union. I honestly thought I was on top of my game. How many other new teachers had teaching experience at a Mexican border town (McAllen, TX, 1995) at WOC-Work Opportunity Center alternative high school in Minneapolis, MN (January of 1994) at an Indian reservation near Leech Lake, MN (summer, 1994) and as a junior/senior high backpack guide at a Bible camp in the Rocky Mountains of Montana at Christikon (the summers 1995 and 1996)? With that resume, I felt primed to handle anything at Caledra Union.

I was so confident in my teaching ability that I shunned my colleague's grading system. I felt homework assignments should be worth more than one point, labs should be worth more than two points, and tests should be worth more than five points. I wanted a system where students could receive partial credit for their work. My colleague's system seemingly put too much emphasis on participation with pass-fail grades. Either the student met the passing criteria or they didn't. The simplified grading system worked well for my coworkers, but it didn't fall in my comfort zone.

Therefore, I established my niche by implementing my own grading system. My system also did not drop the lowest test score, which I knew would cause me to lose favor among students in comparison to all of the teachers that did. The day was going to come where my students would proclaim that half of their grade in other classes comes from extra credit. Not mine. Students were going to have to earn their grade in my class by learning both Latin and Biology.

We live in a society that addresses problems through quick fixes. The over-prescription of drugs is evidence of that. In our schools, the over availability of extra credit similarly serves as a quick fix, especially at the end of a quarter. Grade inflation is not the answer to students' grade woes. There is no way I was going to compromise the integrity of my grading system by offering an end of the semester extra credit project. I was determined to have my students like me without extra credit.

I graduated from a college in southeastern Minnesota the spring of 1995 with a Bachelor of Arts degree and biology major. I didn't commit to the education field until midway through my sophomore year. After graduating in four years, I still had a semester of student teaching practicum and classes to complete. Upon completion, I moved back in with my parents in central, WI, where I spent the spring semester of 1996, substitute teaching in my hometown. There just weren't any full time job listings for biology halfway through the school year.

Substitute teaching gave me a false sense of professional security. The student body LOVED having me as their sub. They liked change. I liked being liked. If only I had heeded the ninety percent of students who said I was nice on their feedback of my aforementioned teaching experiences, I would have realized a premonition of things to come. There is a huge difference between students who respect a teacher versus those who like a teacher.

I remember how fast the first day with students at Caledra Union went. At 3:30 p.m., I was ready to celebrate. My mouth was parched after reading and explaining all thirty of my 'House Rulz' five times over that day. Teaching was easy! The students just sat there and soaked up the 'Rulz'. Yeah, there were a few who dozed off, but all in all, no one teaches in a perfect world. Were all thirty 'Rulz' addressed? Check. Did students finish picking out their seating chart? Check. Was I in groove with the student posse or what? Check. Even Scott Nachtmare in seventh period biology was delighted upon request to have me call him by his nickname, Skippy.

Upon first impression, I considered Scott Nachtmare, a.k.a. 'Skippy,' a pesky little loud-mouthed blonde. He oozed energy; I knew I eventually had to find a way to constructively harness it. Scott playfully commented on everything the first day of school. He was a class clown among his peers.

Anyway, enough about Scott - it was time to celebrate. The first day was a success. I was in.

Why Did I Become a Teacher?

"You will never be rich," my dad said upon hearing me announce my professed career choice. I knew my parents would support my career decision as long as I was happy. I also knew teachers made just enough to pay their bills unless they had the fortune of being married to someone in the white collared world.

Leadership is a prerequisite for being a successful teacher. Growing up, I was a follower, aimlessly searching for my niche, while battling insecurities. Public speaking was never my forte. As a matter of fact, I feared public speaking more than death itself. I was not good at it. Had you seen me nervously preparing for a speech in the waning moments I had before my turn came up in middle school, you might have thought I had Parkinson's disease by the way I shook. My parents told me I just stood silent up on stage playing Joseph during my first children's Christmas program. Some Joseph I was.

Speaking is a left-hemisphere brain dominant skill. I, on the other hand, am right-hemisphere brain dominant. It is the right brain thinkers like me who are gifted in art and music. You should see the quality of my art projects I saved from elementary school. When I engage in public speaking, I talk with my hands, which is an annoying characteristic of right brain thinkers that can serve as a distraction to my audience. While I may possess certain left hemisphere brain dominant traits like analytical thinking and organization, overall, I favor the use of my right hemisphere, which is the reason why public speaking never was natural to me. Science was never naturally easy for me either, as evident by the grades I got in it in elementary and middle school in that subject area.

Traumatizing experiences, like the first piano recital I had at my instructor's house, cemented fear of public speaking and performances into my psyche. At one recital, the neighbor performing before me bolted out of my piano teacher's house in tears after her last song. Before I could comprehend the gravity of the situation, my instructor called me to perform next. I rounded the corner of the hallway and saw nothing but eyes of seated strangers, packed around the piano in my instructor's living room. I thought the older girl before me did a fine job. What was this foreboding adult audience going to do to me? It was then I wished I had practiced more. I dreaded piano recitals as much as I loathed public speaking, but through repeated practice trials, I exorcised my demons and conquered my lack of confidence in public speaking.

When I think of a prototype teacher, an authoritative person who speaks through his eyes comes to mind. In other words, most teachers I know are very good at making direct eye contact with students while they communicate verbally and non-verbally. Then there I am. I was born with the natural tendency to *not* look at my subject directly in the eyes while I speak gene. Maybe it is a survival mechanism passed along through evolution, where my lineage survived by avoiding eye contact with wild predatory animals and later human competitors. I first was made aware of it in ninth grade social studies class, when my teacher called on of my classmates in the audience to evaluate me after my speech. Although I drew high remarks for voice and pacing, the peer evaluator openly ripped on me for looking over their heads and out the window of the classroom the entire duration of my speech.

If you were to carefully study my face now as I speak in public, you periodically will notice my eyelashes flutter. I must posses the same trait as my father-in-law because his eyelashes do that too when he speaks in public. Both of our bodies convey complete calm and collectedness while we speak in public, notwithstanding eyelashes that flutter. They remain a miniature beacon of our nervousness.

How else do I stereotype prototype teachers? They are good at impromptu. They are quick thinkers with spontaneous ideas. I think of them being a natural performer. Someone who would do well in the game show, *Whose Line Is It Anyway*? They are good at promptly defusing any situation that escalates. In my students' current brain personality color activity, the true color of most teachers would be red. My true colors, on the other hand, are green and yellow. I am more of a logical thinker and a planner.

What other attributes of mine undermine my efforts to be the ultimate teacher? When I begin talking, I occasionally stutter in between breaths. I also have a slight lisp at times when I pronounce the letter s. I remember sounding like a hissing snake ten years ago talking into the microphone at a winter awards banquet. How does one conquer both speech impediments? The answer is through painstaking practice. It is one thing to tackle your inner demons as a sadistic past time, but doing it daily and calling it a profession for thirty- five years? I guess it is better than selling Amway products.

Reflecting back on my babysitting adventures during my high school years, I knew then I was not a natural with children. I babysat a lot of spoiled children. Some were respectful and well-mannered; others ran the roost. The latter made games out of calling their mom at work to rat on their siblings behind my back. Surely the thought of having those types of unruly children in my classroom someday would have deterred me from entering the teaching profession, but it didn't.

In college, my academic advisor never told me that many good teachers were misfits themselves in school. Student misfits turned teachers know the working minds of students like their former selves, which enables them to root out discipline problems before they get out of control. On the contrary, I envisioned my future students to be respectful and polite. I idealistically expected all of them to care about their education as much as I did in school. I was the eternal optimist in college.

I recall the day I said good-bye to the undecided undergraduate status and committed to the teaching profession. I was returning to college from an extended Thanksgiving break, cherishing memories spent with the family over the holidays, when I asked myself, why not become a teacher? For the last fourteen years of my life, I have had the summers, weekends, and holidays off. Imagine the world of possibilities during the months of summer and time during the holidays to spend with family. I could meld my science degree with my dainty interest in working with kids. Besides, I wanted to work a profession, not be married to it. Why would I sacrifice everything to go through medical school and residency only to find out at the ripe age of thirty I didn't like being a doctor? What then? I would be enslaved to my employer to pay off my six-figure debt. Teaching made more sense.

Discipline Cycle from Day Two on

School started Tuesday after Labor Day. I naively believed day one went flawless. I lectured the 'House Rulz' until I was blue in the face. It was the old school way to assert classroom control. The problem was constructivist practices succeeded teacher dominated, traditional run classrooms in this generation of hyper-stimulated, attention deficit students. In reality, my students came to the realization they owned me during the forty-eight minute class period on day one. Right away Wednesday, students began talking while I talked. By Friday, the few side bar conversations as I call them flared up all over the room as I stood there in disbelief. Instead of demanding their undivided attention, I talked over them with a louder voice. Before I knew it, the grating side bar conversations became part of daily routine.

My discipline problems got worse. The assistant Principal, Mr. Jonas, eventually paged me for a meeting to discuss my out-of- control classes. The following day, I enforced zero tolerance for unruly behavior and issued out detentions to everyone who talked out of turn. The disciplinary power trip gave me a rush. After a couple of days, the disciplinary assault exhausted me to the point where I didn't have the energies to combat the talking anymore. I learned to pick my fights and disruptive talking no longer remained one of them. I closed the classroom door to masque the noise pollution in my room. My mantra then became 'What happened in biology stayed in biology,' until parents called Mr. Jonas again and pressured him to do something about the chaos in my classroom. A second meeting with Mr. Jonas occurred, and I left motivated again to be a tough teacher, which lasted a couple of days. The cycle repeated itself, and again I found myself teaching behind a closed door-anything to muffle my loud students to any passerby. I taught over the classroom noise to the diminishing number of students who still cared. It was a matter of time before another parental complaint prompted my boss to have another conference with me. This cycle went on for months until Mr. Jonas felt it was time to take drastic intervention measures.

No Excuses for Losing Control

Writing this chapter twelve years after my trials and tribulations at Caledra Union, I shake my head over the opportunity I blew to establish an environment conducive to learning. There were no excuses for losing control of the classes the way I did. Teaching should have been easier back then. For starters, the nationwide divorce rate was lower then in comparison to today, so students should have had more stability, instilled values, and support from their parents. All three attributes should have resulted in all around better students and an easier job description teaching them.

I struggled with foul-mouthed students in a time when the words ass and bitch were still censored over the radio and the major networks on T.V.-unlike today where vulgar expression is commonplace and a decadent influence on our youth. The decline in values at home and in the media over the last decade has made its way into the classroom. More children today habitually swear, and its usage has increased in the hallways and in the classroom. Teachers today continuously tone down foul language, and often help those students express themselves in more appropriate manners. Teachers should be granted English minors for the sheer number of times they expand the vocabulary of students who swear.

More children today disrespectfully talk back to teachers and other adults. School discipline used to precede a second round of discipline from parents. Today an increasing number of parents befriend their child. They accuse the teacher of profiling their child whenever their child gets in trouble. The way our culture embraces violence and rebellion, it's a matter of time before it winds up in classrooms.

In 1996, I had as much technological knowledge as my students, where I at least had a chance to inspire them with use of technology. Forget it nowadays. Power points, as practical as they are, are boring to them. Podcasting and Moodling are the program skill sets that are now taught at the elementary level. In my opinion, both Podcasting and Moodling offer more style than substance, considering the amount of time spent on them. Back then I had a fighting chance to prevent discipline problems through implementation of engaging, technology-based curriculum.

Children in 1996 weren't as lazy back then because they didn't use technology as a crutch. For example, every student I had at Caledra Union could tell time on a hand clock without the help of a digital watch. Not all of today's children have that 'time-honored' ability. Since more students hand wrote assignments back then, I heard fewer technology-based excuses as to why student work was late. Although use of technology has enhanced the quality of projects and saved students considerable amount of time completing them, technological glitches have increasingly caused scores of students to miss their deadlines. Excuses have resulted in students falling academically behind, which put them at risk to become apathetic and prone to cause discipline problems. Lesser dependence on technology in my starting year of 1996 should have translated into fewer excuses, which should have resulted in better grades and more attachment to the class. Technology-based excuses that plague students more so now than then are:

- "Filters didn't let me access data sites for research"

- "Instead of using class time to start a written assignment, I'll wait (procrastinate) and do the assignment later on the computer"

- "I thought I saved my work on the server, but didn't"

- "My printer at home doesn't work"

- "My computer at home crashed"

- "I was on pass restriction so I couldn't go to the library to work on the computers there or check out a lap top"

- "The high school computer lab was locked and I couldn't get my printout in on time"

- "I printed out my document through the printer in the high school office and when I went there to pick it up, it wasn't there"

- "I couldn't save my work because I forgot to log on correctly"

- "I couldn't print because the printer was out of toner"

- "It's not my fault spell check didn't catch all of these grammatical errors!"

- "The server was too slow"

- Caught on e-mail, My Space, Facebook, playing D.J. or playing computer games during class work time

More children today expect immediate gratification and success without first earning it through hard work. They expect to be passed on through social promotion by just showing up to class. Years of ego protection and coddling have made many of today's students spoiled brats who obstinately insist on doing everything their way. An expectation is now placed on teachers to meet students' learning needs versus expecting students to adapt to different teaching styles. We are destined to make life easy for the students when we should be teaching them adaptation skills for survival in the job market.

I remember having butterflies in my stomach every year in elementary school the spring morning my teacher announced whether we were going to be held back. As a proficient student, I never was given an advanced promise that I would be promoted. Promotion to me was an earned right of passage.

Students' attitudes today are different. They expect to be passed on regardless of whether they exert any effort to learning. They do not harbor an inner unsettling feeling that their deficiencies will cause them to be held back. Consequentially, corporations outsource jobs overseas because a growing percentage of the American work force lacks ambition, drive, and dependability because *educators are pressured to graduate them that way.*

In summary, teaching should have been easier my first year in 1996. I offer no excuses for my trials and tribulations. I am left with the disgusted feeling that I blew a golden opportunity to start out my career on a good note.

Mitch Sinclair

Meet Mitch. He was a freshman in my first period physical science class with a third grade reading level. No one told me in college I would be teaching classes with students that would be six grade levels behind in reading. Not just reading, but reading comprehension. To make matters worse, the scientific jargon made the reading level of the physical science textbooks college level. I was overwhelmed brainstorming ways to teach such an abstract curriculum to him with an extremely low ability.

I had no plan in place to differentiate the curriculum because I was never trained to differentiate in college. I didn't receive that training until grad school four years later. How does one make accommodations without lowering expectations for a student six grade levels behind?

Assigning students of disproportionate ability to a teacher in a classroom is a senseless, time-honored tactic. The public relation term is inclusion, where teachers perform magic to ensure no child is left behind. Why don't doctors improve their efficiency by seeing thirty patients, all with different conditions at once? Sounds senseless, but that is the unrealistic expectation placed upon teachers. It is possible teachers are the most gifted professionals for even attempting to simultaneously meet the diverse needs of their students.

It would be an interesting juxtaposition to see how effective Vince Lombardi would be at teaching high school today. Mr. Lombardi was a consummate professional, with a pedagogical style like none other. Long before he became the legendary coach of the Green Bay Packer teams that won five NFL Championships in a nine-year span[1], he coached and taught physics, chemistry, and Latin at St. Cecilia, a small Catholic high school in New Jersey [2]. He pounded out each lesson by rote until the slowest kid in the room understood it and the reasons why it was so [3]. Did Mr. Lombardi differentiate his curriculum to best meet the needs of both gifted students and those with low ability? No, yet he later became arguably one of the most successful and storied coaches in NFL history.

Teachers today wish they had time in class to pound the lesson into students' heads until the slowest person got it. If we indoctrinated Mr. Lombardi's pedagogy, I think the gifted students would die of boredom from redundancy. They too, along with teachers, would get mad at their apathetic peers. Motivating every student in class to learn is unheard of in today's world. As a 21st Century education-related proverb goes, "If no child gets ahead, then no child will be left behind!"

I didn't know much about physical science. It had been a decade since I last had taken the course as an eighth grader. I was not even certified to teach physical science-only grades 7-12 life science. Actually, the Department of Public Instruction informed me a year after leaving Caledra that I only had a long-term substitute license for the life sciences in the state of

Wisconsin. I eventually learned I was fully licensed to teach life science in the state of Minnesota, which is where I graduated from college, but the state of Wisconsin required three more courses totaling eight credits in order for me to be fully certified. Regardless of my credentials, the administrative personnel at Caledra probably felt I had taken enough general science college credits to teach remedial physical science first period.

Poor Mitch had to weather the storm of expectations I laid out for everyone. By golly, if his special education teacher felt he was capable of being mainstreamed into a regular education classroom with no modifications written in his Individualized Education Plan, then so be it. I was going to treat Mitch like everyone else.

Despite my pessimism for Mitch's chances at the outset of the year, he proved me wrong. Mitch didn't just survive, he excelled. He finished the year with an A-. In a year marred with student rebellion, I marveled at all of his attributes, in particular his courtesy, obedience, and work ethic. His all out effort did more than impress me-it raised the bar for my expectations of future students with disabilities. If a freshman with a third grade reading level could excel in my class without modification, so should all others with lesser disabilities. Mitch worked extra hard to overcome his limitations.

From this point on, I would not accept future excuses of laziness as a disability. I won't be impressed with special ed. students who use their notes to score better on tests than their regular ed. classmates. I will scoff at special education teachers who take the test for their children in a resource room. I will disrespect special education teachers who show up at my door for the first time the *last week of the semester* saying, "We have to do something about so and so's grade."

The only hang-up I had teaching physical science was that all of the students took the same class a year ago as eighth graders. After their eighth grade promotion, they signed up for the easiest high school science credit they could find, which happened to be physical science-again. Nothing I taught was new-it was all review. They had already seen the outcomes of many of the demonstrations I conducted for them, even though they couldn't explain to me squat about what they were supposed to learn from those same experiences a year ago. I learned that some of the lower level science teachers showcase the frills of science demonstrations without teaching the substance that should accommodate them.

In Trouble with the Custodians

I strolled into the science office area one brisk October morning when Marcy, the secretary, halted me in my tracks.

"Mr. Parker," she said, "you are to report immediately to the custodial office. They didn't sound very happy with you."

I took a moment to process the negative undertones of her urgent message. Why would the janitors be mad at me? There went my goal at the beginning of the year of being on good social graces with them. I paused to consider why they were upset with me. Then it dawned on me-the calorimeter lab yesterday! My students left the lab area a mess, with ashes of burned food morsels all over the floor. <Gulp>. I meant to tidy it up after school but got waylaid in the process.

The calorimeter lab kicked off the cell chemistry unit. Students used the recorded change in both the food mass and water temperature to determine the calories in each morsel of food. From there, they calculated the macromolecule content of carbohydrates, lipids, and protein in each food item. My students had a heyday in lab, making a bloody mess with ashen matches and food morsels.

"Where again is the custodial office?" I inquired.

"Take the right hallway around the commons and it will be the first door on the left," She directed.

A minute later I cautiously knocked on the semi-ajar door of their office. A man and woman custodian greeted me with a beleaguered glare from the opposite end of the room. She was leaning up against the counter with her arms folded, guarding the coffee machine.

"I am, um, Steve Parker, the person I believe you wanted to see." With my luck, maybe they were seeking someone else. Their continued stare dispelled that notion.

"Do you have any idea how long it took us to clean your room last night?" She bristled.

"Um, no," I swallowed.

"An hour and a half," she scowled, transitioning into a silent glare. I waited in uncomfortable silence for her to continue.

"We are on a tight schedule here," she seethingly lipped.

"Listen, I am sorry. I obviously am new here, and am still learning the ropes. It was not my intention for my lab to get out of hand. I probably should be counting my blessings that my students didn't burn down the school," I mumbled in reply.

They were not in the mood for humor. Quick, think of something to say Steve to show them that you understand the gravity of the situation. Since I didn't envision another lab as potentially messy as this one, I said in closure, "I won't let it happen again," and left them with their coffee.

If I Were an Advanced Placement Teacher for a Day

Everything was running smoothly, until it began-a muffled, flapping sound broke the code of silence. It resonated from the overhead ventilation system, getting closer and becoming louder, until it appeared. I could not believe my eyes. Here I was proctoring an Advanced Placement exam the year before, and a wild songbird forged its way into the conference testing room, flying like a bat out of hell! The European starling frantically flew around, bludgeoning itself as it repeatedly tried to fly through the windows. The test was put into abeyance as we evacuated the room until the bird was captured and released. Try explaining that occurrence to the AP headquarters!

I sat at my desk nestled in Caledra Union's science department office area and the clock read 9:45 a.m. Only five minutes remained of my prep period. I couldn't help but notice how well behaved the students in Garrett Speaker's Advanced Placement Biology class was through the adjacent doorway. I could clearly hear Mr. Speakers facilitate a review. Whenever he paused his discourse, you could have heard a pin drop on the floor. The tranquility of his classroom was opposite the chaos in mine. I wheeled my chair over to the edge of the doorway and peeked in. I drooled in envy over what I observed. Mr. Speakers had complete control of his class. His presence commanded the respect of his students.

The bell rang and I passed through his class en route to mine. "It must be nice teaching mature upperclassmen who want to be here." I commented to Mr. Speakers.

"Quite contrary. A number of my students don't want to be here. They signed up for my class only because their parents made them," he answered.

I interpreted Mr. Speaker's reply as a conditioned response that downplayed how rosy his job description was. Whom are you trying to kid, teaching honors classes all day? I guess if you paid your dues over the years teaching basic level science courses, then I suppose you have earned the right to challenge the best upper level students the school had to offer in your elective classes.

I momentarily dreamt of being Mr. Speaker for a day with a full palate of honors classes. It seemed teaching Advanced Placement was a rite of passage for veteran teachers. They work with a low teacher-student ratio. They spend their energies toward challenging young minds versus wasting it on motivation. Advanced Placement teachers like him inherit the intrinsically motivated, the cream of the crop, the responsible upper classmen. Classroom management would not be a concern.

Teaching has to be so much easier when students actually let you teach.

I called Mr. Speaker's bluff that morning, but in retrospect I don't think he was bluffing when he said many of his students were misplaced, having signed up for the wrong reasons. I agreed with his comment on misplacement because I regretted taking an Advanced Placement course in high school. My concerns about the Advanced Placement program had nothing to do with the quality of my former instructor, because he was one of the premier teachers in my high school.

All things considered, I will play Devil's advocate to air my concerns about Advanced Placement (AP) for argument's sake. In response to a variety of pressures, I believe public schools herd a growing annual number of students into AP courses. In light of that, I wonder how many parents fully understand how many negative ramifications there potentially are from pressuring their children to take AP courses for which they may not be prepared.

Students taking Advanced Placement courses are susceptible to burn out. Adding college curriculum to a high school schedule where students are in class all day potentially leaves inadequate time for a well-rounded student to study. Teenagers are only in high school once. Many adults think children of today are growing up too fast, skipping adolescence, as kids fast forward from childhood into adulthood. High school is the last chance for kids to be kids. It is also the last chance for them to take electives for free. Some Advanced Placement students focus on one subject area too prematurely without allowing themselves an opportunity to explore other paths. Valuable life skills are taught in elective courses, like cooking or the auto mechanics. These same courses often are the ones AP students cannot fit into their schedules. If high school alumni do not know how to cook, or change the oil in their car, then we are graduating individuals who are too dependent on the service sector of our society.

Students also are more likely to discover secondary interests and career pathways if they opt to take electives in lieu of Advanced Placement. Some teenagers that take AP prematurely narrow down their career choice with expensive consequences down the road. It is a lot cheaper for those students to change their mind about their career path in high school than it is for them to do so in college.

Some advocates for Advanced Placement argue that the program whittles down the number of years it takes the participating student to graduate college. The main reason why it takes many college freshmen six years to graduate is _not_ due to a lack of academic rigor in high school by avoiding Advanced Placement courses; rather, it is because underclassmen in college get the worst draw time for scheduling, which throws off their tracking. If they are unable to matriculate in prerequisite courses they need because all of the sections are closed, then that will extend the timeline it takes for them to complete the sequence of courses they need for that major, and to graduate. The timeline will further be extended if they change majors.

Another reservation I have about pushing the Advanced Placement program arises from the teaching side of the spectrum. I am a teacher, not a lecturer. Teaching is a relative term, because there is a distinct difference between teaching information and telling it. Most college professors _tell_ the curriculum vitae to their students in a lecture hall with the expectation their students will learn it on their own. If I expected my students to learn the core subject matter independently, then what would they need me for?

In spite of my qualms, I think Advanced Placement is the right program for a select, gifted few. Taking AP does teach independent learning skills, and even if the student fails to earn college credits, the AP class will inevitably help the high school student when he retakes the course in college. For the record, I think every student should be given the opportunity to take AP courses. If students should happen to fail without discouragement, it is best they were given the chance to do so in the first place.

Tobacco Row

"Becky, what is copied in transcription?"

"Huh?"

"Surely you can take a break from your chatter and join our review session," I advised pointedly. I repeated the question about protein synthesis to her in my fifth period biology class.

"DNA."

"And the copied strand is called?" I turned, continuing my query with, "Mark?"

He just stared at me. His impish grin belied, "Go ahead and wait for my answer. I have no clue, so you might as well stop wasting everyone's time in asking me."

"m-RNA," Olivia blurted, out of turn.

I turned to her, relieved that someone knew the answer, but I fumed at her crass way of undermining my review. I thought, "I can't check for understanding if students impulsively bail out their peers and answer on their behalf."

"m-RNA. You are correct. The 'm' stands for?" I continued, turning to face... "Kylee?"

Kylee lifted her bored head off the folded arms on her desk to mutter, "Messenger."

"Good." I rounded Mark's aisle into the next one over, in hopes my proximity control would keep enough order to facilitate a review over the rude chatter. Why aren't these students taking my class seriously? My troubled worry suddenly took a backseat to the gross chew-filled gob of spit on the floor halfway down the next aisle. The attentive students immediately knew from my double take something unusual grabbed my attention.

The gob of spit decorated a floor tile next to Seth's desk. I had to make a split second decision as to whether the spit was fresh and not from a perpetrator in third period, which would have preceded this class. I quickly ruled that out option B and confronted Seth.

"Forget your spit can today Seth?"

After a second-long evil eye standoff, Seth shifted his blank stare straight ahead of him.

"Open your mouth and show me the inside lining of your gums." I ordered. Seconds passed as the class watched in suspended animation.

"I have all day," I persistently nagged with a twinge of irritation. Seth continued to stare straight ahead with a sudden case of lockjaw.

"Actually, I don't have all day. Either open your mouth now or go to the office."

"This is bullshit!" He lashed out, vacating his seat.

"You have been sucking on that all hour!" I answered wryly with the knowledge that shit is one of the ingredients in chewing tobacco.

Seth received a detention for insubordination. The administration was never able to prove he chewed tobacco in my class that day. In all likelihood he swallowed the evidence, and later went home sick because of it. I was reminded of how some high school students will do anything to detach from reality, even if it means abusing their indestructible bodies.

Dodging a Bullet

Luck was on my side the day Mrs. Stenbaugh, the executive principal, walked into my fourth period biology classroom unannounced to observe me the last week in October. Mrs. Stenbaugh randomly picked the only class I had a legitimate shot at impressing her.

To this day, I dislike having visitors in my classroom. Students are too easily distracted with their puny attention spans. They act differently in the presence of guests.

Luckily for me, most of my students were attentive and engaged during the observation. The few misfits that accounted for the usual disruptive hum in that class must have been too tired that day to cause mayhem. I was so relieved at the end of the observation, because I knew I dodged a bullet.

The follow up appointment with Mrs. Stenbaugh gave me reason to celebrate. She was satisfied with my overall performance! I finally received a positive memo to grace my personnel file. Mrs. Stenbaugh did not deal directly with disciplinary issues, and therefore did not know my struggles this fall. She never attended my pressure-cooked meetings over classroom management with the two assistant principals at the high school. This was one of the few moments I valued the bureaucracy of a school district this big, where discipline struggles that befell me daily wasn't a concern to the evaluator who should have known about it the most.

Despite the sensation of relief, my stomach remained unsettled. I had one observation down and one to go. The odds were not in my favor Mrs. Stenbaugh would pick this fourth period biology class again. I had no realistic chance of impressing her with my teaching ability in any of my other classes.

The shit will hit the fan when she sees how dire my situation is-that is, if she doesn't hear about it first through the grapevine. Students in my first period physical science would not be vocally rude to me, but I know she won't be impressed to find them half asleep. I could envision her evaluative notes from a first period class visit. Mr. Parker is a fraud. He is uninspiring, and needs to take a class on motivation.

How about scenario two, where Mrs. Stenbaugh shows up unannounced in my seventh period biology class? Have you ever wished a student would move out of the district to make your life easier? Well, I had one of those students in seventh period biology. His name was Scott Nachtmare. He was an obnoxious little snot-a monger for being the center of attention. His impish smiles beget trouble daily. The only chance I had of having an impressive unannounced observation seventh period was if Scott was home sick that day.

I never believed one student had the wherewithal and ability to ruin a class until I met

Scott. Analogically speaking, if the rot from one cob of corn can spread and ruin a bushel, then yes. Some of Scott's classmates learned how to tune him out over the years, like that referee in the commercial who is able to tune out yelling coaches during games because he had conditioned himself to tune out his wife, who chronically screamed in his ears at home. Other classmates of Scott validated his antics on a daily basis. They found solace in his amusement at the expense of a subject area they could care less about.

Then there was Michelle, a classmate of Scott's seventh period, who was visibly torn. You could tell she tried to serve two masters. She superficially chummed with Scott for social acceptance, while deep down worried about being a good student who was supposed to get good grades to make her parents happy. Michelle tried to respectfully maintain eye contact with me throughout the lesson, but her grand plan to learn was hijacked by the devil himself - Scott. His snickering comments chinked away at her façade of undivided attention. She smiled at him, giggled with him, whispered back to him, and sometimes slapped him. If Michelle were Catholic, I hope for her sake she booked back-to-back sessions each week in the confessional booth to atone for her sins as Scott's sidekick accomplice.

Moving on to other nightmarish possibilities of Mrs. Stenbaugh showing up unannounced in a class other than fourth period, I had to consider scenario three, a visit to my fifth period biology class. Fifth period was noisy. That's what happens when the boy to girl ratio is four to one, which was the case for that period. There was way too much testosterone in there. Did the guidance counselor who scheduled this class have a clue? Seemingly every study on gender differences in learning suggests males have shorter attention spans, and therefore need to learn through hands-on activities. Forget the passive learning environment that so many old school administrators prefer. As they walk down the halls, they think teachers with good discipline teach in classrooms where the passerby hears one voice emanating from the room-the teacher's. Students are not to be heard, because they should be quietly taking notes while the teacher lectures. Well, that was before the constructivist movement took off and today's generation of teachers became trained to be more of a classroom facilitator, where students actively learn from each other in a noisier setting.

To top it off, I played the savior the second week of school and let veteran colleague, Mrs. Campbell, sweet talk her way into transferring Kyle, her two week-old problem student, over to my fifth period biology class. I was so naïve to think I could do a better job of connecting with him.

My fifth period students were disrespectfully noisy, but I became conditioned to it, just as the residents do who live near train tracks. A seating chart wouldn't have helped at this stage in the game. There were too many chattery friends in that class to separate. The ringleader was Greg Vinoli.

Then I pondered scenario four. Mrs. Stenbaugh shows up unannounced in my eighth period biology class. That would be an ultimate nightmare. I would rather have students point out to me during class that my fly is wide open. I would even prefer to find myself stalked by Jason on Friday the 13th. If Mrs. Stenbaugh were to enter the eighth period war zone, it would be the end of my teaching tenure at Caledra Union. I would be sent into the abyss of teacher corrective in-services.

Mrs. Idacky, a colleague who taught biology next door to me, was fully aware of my notorious eighth period class. One day she said to me in passing, "They aren't giving you a chance (to teach)."

Wow, what words of comfort. She hit the nail on the head. My eighth period students weren't giving me a chance. It was the gossipy girls in there who never shut up. They talked all hour. Every one of their conversations during class ate away at my dignity. There was a remote chance I could get their undivided attention if I started off the lesson by saying, "Today we are going to learn about the penis."

My eighth period boys talked at will too, but their rationale was different. They did it to spite me. They lost utter respect for me, because I singled them out for talking and disciplined them. It became a parity issue. They were the scapegoats. I'm not sure why it was so hard for me to discipline the girls. Maybe the boys' lower pitched voices irritated me more. My inattentiveness toward the rude girls may have also been attributed to a huge blind spot similar to what I experienced while batting in little league baseball. Regardless, I wasn't concerned about the culmination of my mistakes at this point, a third of the way through the school year. I was in survival mode. This was the class where I easily entertained the notion of sending half of the students to the principal's office.

One of my most regretful moments occurred at fall parent teacher conference. Melanie from eighth hour surprised me by showing up to conferences with her mom. I did not have the guts to tell her mom the ugly truth of how disrespectful her daughter was in class. I cowardly said, "Melanie needs to do a better job paying attention in class."

Melanie was one of several talkative children in class. The talking all hour became a blur. I no longer kept track of who talked and when. Mr. Jonas, the assistant principal, was right in saying to me that I couldn't effectively teach if I was too preoccupied disciplining my students. I adapted to the direness of the situation. I turned my attention on throwing a lifeline to the few students who cared. Survival was about focusing on the positives. The day would come when I would have a brand new start, and a second chance.

I prayed every night for the strength to tough the year out. I had to keep this class under the radar until June eleventh. If only the concrete walls were more soundproof. If only Mrs. Stenbaugh would magically revisit and observe fourth period biology again. Better yet, if only her satisfaction of me from her first observation would cause her to exempt me the second time around.

All that mattered to me was my personal file finally had a beacon of light in the form of a satisfactory evaluation of my job performance. It spelled out H-O-P-E for my summer job interviews. I lost control of this class the day after I bored them to sleep monotonously reading the thirty 'House Rulz.' On my way to losing this class, I quickly learned that handing out detentions was an ineffective way to curb student misconduct.

I was a marked man, receiving pressure from parents, administrators, and colleagues to improve the learning environment in my classes. Beleaguered and cynical, I knew it was impossible for me to accomplish this at this juncture of the school year. Don't they know that once you lose control of a class, you will _NEVER_ get it back?

Scott Nachtmare

All of my students had finished their lab and were seated for the post-lab discussion, except for Scott. He discreetly stepped out of his shoes and went shoeless at the start of lab, only to find his shoes at the end of lab drenched with water in the bottom of a lab sink. Here I was, trying to facilitate the post lab discussion, and there was Scott, adamant about slapping the soles of his wet shoes onto the edge of the lab table in efforts to dry them off, without an end in sight.

Most days, Scott made racket with his loud mouth during discussion. He was the very reason why I never gave out participation points in discussion. He dominated class discussion for the attention of getting off topic.

Today, however, wasn't a loquacious game for him. His mind was on vengeance, not on my question as to why he took off his shoes in the first place.

Scott glowered, "I am going to kill the person who did this!"

"Scott, let's discuss this matter after class. Please return to your seat."

"I can't believe this happened!" he yelled defiantly, continuing to make the shoe-slapping racket.

"Scott, the class is waiting for you to sit down so we can proceed with the lesson. Please sit down and take care of that later."

"No! Why should I? I did nothing wrong!"

"Scott, you can go to the office!"

"No, why should I?"

"Now."

"No!" he hollered, still slapping his shoes on the lab countertop.

I waited impatiently, unable to call the office because I didn't have a phone in the room. The melee in the classroom attracted the attention of a passerby teacher in the hallway. The timing of his intervention was impeccable. The tall, authoritative male Phys. Ed. teacher stepped into the room and pointedly commanded, "Come with me now!" Scott's disgusted gasp resonated across the room.

"FINE, I will leave for him…but not for you, you *HELL-BOUND HOMO!*" He screamed.

I was shaken and figuratively in shock. Scott had finally vacated the premises, but not before he got the best of me. He won the battle and made me look like a fool. Bleary-eyed, I broke the silence and uttered, "I just want to teach." I was an emotional wreck the remainder of the day. There I was, Mr. Teacher, crying in front of my bewildered students. Tears or not, I had an unfinished job to do.

After school I retreated to my desk. Our office area was still a mess from the renovation as was my life. I needed a few moments to myself before heading off to basketball practice. I was the freshman girls' basketball coach at Caledra Union. It was a blessing for me to work with freshmen girls that did not witness my embarrassing clash with Scott.

I scurried home after practice. Home for me was a spare bedroom I rented from Ben Salari – an earth science teacher at Caledra Union. After checking and seeing there were no new telephone messages from family or school, I erased the dozen week-old messages on the answering machine. Ben, my landlord, later reamed me out for deleting them because he wanted message three saved. I finished my social responsibilities that demoralizing day with a sincere apology to Ben. Tired and jaded, I retreated upstairs and took a long hot shower. After dressing in my night garb, I curled up on my futon, my makeshift bed, and cried myself to sleep while praying for a better tomorrow.

The following day, I received a letter of encouragement from one of my fourth hour students. The paraphrased letter, dated December 4th, 1996, read as follows:

Mr. Parker,

I am really sorry to hear about what happened yesterday during seventh hour biology. I am incredibly disappointed in how immature some of my punk-like classmates can be. I wanted to write this letter on behalf of a majority of your students. You are a nice person and a great teacher. Please don't change your attitude about your good students because we have an overwhelming amount of faith and respect for you and the way you teach. My test scores show it. Keep your faith in us; the next time an incident like this occurs, we will continue to support you. Take care,

-Vagas Smiley & your students

        Sadly, I had no time to find solace in Vaga's letter of encouragement because my confrontations soon continued with Scott, this time over the missing status of his friend Nancy's lab report. He defiantly claimed she turned her report in on time and that he *saw* her turn it in. Unfortunately for Nancy, I didn't trust him. There was no grade recorded for her on that assignment in the gradebook. I didn't remember seeing it among the eighty other lab reports I recently had graded. Instead of giving Nancy the benefit of the doubt, I asked her to show me her graded work. She then confessed to me she didn't save it. Running out of words to say, Nancy was on the verge of tears.

        "But I *SAW* her turn it in! I *know* she turned it in!" Scott bellowed. Scott wasted no time escalating the situation. He acted like a champion among his peers standing up for fellow student rights against the big, evil teacher. He then threw up his arms in a temper tantrum, accusing me of losing Nancy's lab report. Nancy stared off in the distance, dejected. Scott continued his tirade, looking to spar with me. He once again became the center for attention while disrupting the lesson.

This was one of those moments I wished one of my thirty 'House Rulz' at the beginning of the year required students to save all of their returned, graded assignments. I could not comprehend why students so proud of their graded work would hastily throw it away upon return. On second thought, maybe it's because we live in a throw away society.

No matter how bad I wanted to exempt Nancy from that lab grade, I simply could not give students the benefit of the doubt. I had gotten burned a month earlier letting seemingly honest students take attendance for me. Some of conniving volunteers marked their truant friends present, which caused me to get into hot water with the administration.

I was convinced Nancy lost her paper and that Scott was out to make me the scapegoat. Being organized, I harbored no history of losing students' work. I told her outright that she was responsible for not saving her work. Unbeknownst to her to this day, her paper finally surfaced after the quarter ended. It had accidentally become lodged in the cordoned off section of my red gradebook.

I still occasionally fail to record a student's grade fourteen years into the teaching profession. When you grade over two thousand assignments a quarter, chances are you will accidentally omit a few of the grade entries-for whatever reason. Sometimes assignments completed on frayed notebook paper cling together, causing oversight. Some teachers ban that writing medium for that reason. Other times students who habitually forget to sign their name on their work forget to check their grades, until the nameless paper is thrown out of the lost and found. Proprietors of the discarded papers later become mad, and blame the teacher for "losing" their work. Sometimes students hand their paper to me instead of the "in" basket while I am in the middle doing something else. Then absent-mindedly, I stash their work in a forgettable, unconventional place. In hindsight, that is what happened to Nancy's paper. I eventually found her graded lab sheet buried in the bowels of my gradebook at the end of the school year. Notwithstanding, Scott was sent to the office for his failure to defuse. Right or wrong, Scott awaited detention for becoming confrontational. I wasn't going to be his verbal punching bag the rest of the class period. I had a lesson to teach.

One day after school, I happened to walk by the detention room. Curious to know which of my students were serving, I back peddled and glanced in. I then saw *him*, Scott, sitting three desks back, two rows from the door. I knew the administration issued him a detention from an occurrence in my class earlier in the week, but I was oblivious as to when he had to serve it. Scott angrily stared *through* the open literature book that was propped up in front of him. His mouth was clenched shut with purled lips. I could feel his anger and sense a vendetta broiling through his flushed red skin. I was very careful not to make my presence known to him at the edge of the doorway. I momentarily was creeped out after having seen the remake of *Cape Fear* starring Robert DeNiro.

For the first time, I wished schools would abolish the senseless past practice of letting students in detention do homework, because it wasn't effective. All Scott did was furtively vent his anger. Even if Scott used the time in detention to do his homework, then schools are teaching students that doing schoolwork is a punishment. Learning in school should be a privilege, not a consequence. A better alternative, albeit idealistic, would be to make students in detention give back to the school or to society. Have them clean lockers, desktops, dry erase boards, or pick up litter off of school grounds-anything that does not directly benefit them. Allowing Scott to read Hamlet in detention will never teach him the magnitude of damage he inflicted on my classroom walls.

Scott likely left detention later that afternoon believing *I* gave him detention because I hated him. He very well may have left with the premise he did nothing wrong in the first place, and that he was a victim of being profiled. That afternoon I may have walked away from the battlefield victorious because he served time, but in the end, the war was clearly his.

One gorgeous afternoon in early April, I took my seventh period biology class sans Scott out to the school forest for a lesson on ecology. Scott was serving the first of a three-day in school suspension for vandalizing the walls from hardened spit wads of legendary proportions. After having my classroom walls assaulted from Scott's newfound past time, I finally had caught him in the act. The spit wad that incriminated him was made from chewing on an entire sheet of notebook paper.

I looked forward to the next few days of teaching without Scott. My confession sounds awful; I was just being honest. My vacation from Scott was short lived when I saw Mr. Jonas escorting him towards me as I ushered my class back to the building from the adjacent school forest. It looked like Mr. Jonas had a vice-like grip on Scott's upper arm. We met up on the walkway next to the tennis courts. I directed my class to proceed to the building so they wouldn't be late for eighth period. Scott made a last minute ditch effort to join up with his friends with a fleeting turnabout, but got nowhere with Mr. Jonas as his shackle. A vice-like tug on Scott's arm brought him back to reality.

"I believe you have something to say to Mr. Parker," Mr. Jonas prodded. Scott bared nothing but his left cheek to me. "Scott," he repeated sternly.

"Mum srry," Scott uttered, with his head fixated on the ground.

"Say it to Mr. Parker," Mr. Jonas demanded.

The punk paused for a second to mull over his options. This time in a more audible voice he said, "Sorry."

"That will be all," Mr. Jonas said to me. "Let's go Scott." I stood there, shaking my head.

He couldn't even look me in the eye during the apology. You had good intentions Mr. Jonas, but Scott's contrived half-assed apology was a waste of my time.

The school year was 1996-1997. Bush emerged onto the rock scene with the hit song "Greedy Fly". Alannis Morisette and Jewel became permanent fixtures on the pop station airwaves. The Green Bay Packers steamrolled most of their opponents en route to becoming Super Bowl XXXI champions in 1997. Atlanta was recovering from hosting the Summer Olympics. Then there was the burgeoning popularity of the Simpsons. One of the most student-quoted catch phrases of Bart Simpson was "Aye Karumba." When Scott, my least favorite student, began using that cliché, I permanently disliked the Simpsons from that moment on.

Let's talk about you, Bart Simpson imitator, Scott Nachtmare. You were my headache-inducing nightmare. You turned your peers against me and gained fanfare for it. My classroom became your playground for attention. You were loud and obnoxious. I personally don't care if you had partial hearing loss and were loud to compensate for it. Nothing excused you for your problematic behavior. There wasn't enough room in class for both of us. You won from the get-go.

Seven months later, I was advised to give up the reigns to my seventh period class with Scott. I took a pay cut for it, but more importantly, I was stripped of my dignity. I considered myself a failure, reaching the abyss of the teaching profession. I was so relieved to say I was done teaching when the final bell rang in June. Losing control of four classes became nine months of sheer hell. The only thing that remotely compares to it on a milder degree is being a parent and losing control of your children for fifteen plus years. I wish neither occurrence on anybody-ever.

Upon my demotion, Scott was transferred to a different section with Mrs. Idacky. He went on to receive another in school suspension, this time with her, which gave me relief to know that Scott was the problem, not me. I hoped the administration made note of that. It wasn't just me who had trouble with him. I firmly believed Scott needed intervention in an alternative school.

I lost count over how many detentions Scott received from his altercations with me. It was pretty obvious the way schools run detentions does nothing to curb student misconduct. Heck, if you were to ask most students in detention how they got there, they either would say, "I don't know why," or "The teacher doesn't like me." In an idealistic world, the outcome of all detentions would parallel the feel-good story of self-discovery as was portrayed in the movie the *Breakfast Club*.

I'm not sure if any form of detention would have made a difference with Scott, but I will guarantee you one thing. I will never name my baby Scott. The list of turn off names from past, current, and future troublemakers in the classroom makes naming babies difficult to do if you are a teacher. If you like me are married to another teacher, then this task becomes mission impossible.

Excuses

Students tested me my first year with an array of excuses as to why they didn't get their homework done and/or why they failed.

- "I don't care" [often drug related apathy]

- "You (the teacher) don't like me"

- "I don't like you (the teacher)"

- [Hyperbole] "Everyone else is failing!" (If enough of us fail, it's the teacher's fault)

- "How is this class going to help me?"

- "I didn't know I had to turn this in or save my work for a semester portfolio/capstone project." (I didn't listen)

- "I don't need this credit to graduate. I'm just taking this class as an elective."

- "The teachers all hate me, and my parents believe it so they have written excuses for me to skip out of school" (pseudo-truancy)

- "I don't like the students in this class"

- ZZZZZZZZZZZZ

- Missing assignments

- "The school will pass me onto the next grade level even with two F's like it did last year" (social promotion)

- "My parents didn't need good grades in school to get high paying jobs, so why do I need them?"

- "I was absent that lesson. Why should I have to make it up? Why am I being tested on it?"

- "I'll work for my parents when I turn 18, regardless of my grades"

- "I intend to fail regular biology and switch over to basic biology next year" (the student wrongly assumes that lowering one's standards will justify an approved easier schedule)

- "I want to fail and flunk out of school so the court orders me to live with my cool dad over in his district"

- "I want to fail my senior year so I can stay in school to be with my younger girlfriend"

- "My mom makes me attend school so she can collect her social security check"

- "I couldn't pass this class even if I did try" (confidence issue)

- "I can't do the work; I'm pregnant!"

The Promised Land

'Twas the weekend before Christmas and all throughout Caledra, many creatures were stirring, especially in the pubs. Ben Salari, my landlord and coworker, and I made sure of it. Tonight, the spirits abounded to a younger than usual crowd because the seasonally festive pub was packed with alumni home from college. One alumnus after another came up to Ben and reminisced over the good times they had in school together. The professional boundaries were down. Tonight, Mr. Salari was Ben. Everyone was an adult now. I envied how many teenagers Ben inspired in the six years he had been teaching.

"Could somebody please pass the pitcher?" I queried. Maybe my next glass of beer would drown out my envy.

I envisioned being in Ben's shoes, with my former pupils reacquainting with me. I longed to hear about their future growth and maturity. I desired to know how well I prepared them for college. What was review for them? What science content area did they struggle with? What suggestions would they have to help make me a better teacher? I drank to all of the promising thoughts and future feedback I was to someday receive.

"Who needs a refill?" announced Richard, a fellow teacher, with the pitcher hoisted mightily in the air. My half-empty mug flagged his attention.

Ben and his former students continued to laugh as they reconnected. The stories aired and got raunchier as the night wore on. I longed to someday hear the tell-all confessions of naughty things my students got away with in my class without ever getting caught. The booze was kicking in, and the place was humming.

"It must be an honor to have former students take time away from their long-lost friends to say hello to you," I wistfully pondered. The fact these alumni remember Ben after only having him as a teacher one year is testimony that he was an inspiration to them. This is my only year at Caledra Union due to the limitation of my one-year contract. I won't be around to see the fruits of my labor five to ten years from now. That's too bad. There are many I would want to see.

You aren't in heaven if you are a spectator to it. I was a visitor in Mr. Salari's promised land. I watched Ben reap what he sowed as a teacher. He savored the moment. In a town of over thirty thousand, the alumni remembered him because he made a difference, and that is what education is all about.

At the very least, it felt great to finally be on the same playing field as my fellow teachers. No one cared I was the weakest link of Caledra's science staff. What mattered was our love for beer this festive occasion.

Parker Versus Idacky

I was busy grading papers at my office cubicle when Mrs. Idacky, a fellow biology teacher, stormed up to me.

"Where did you get that file?"

Startled, I frantically gazed at the document in front of me, while processing my displeasure of her sucker punch accusation.

"From a desktop folder on our science secretary's computer, where our science department collectively keeps our files online," I responded.

"You *do* know this is *my* document. You just can't go stealing other people's work. What were you thinking?"

"I honestly didn't know you were the proprietor. I assumed that since we lesson planned together and shared activities, that this particular lesson was science department domain. It's not like I accessed your file folder with a stolen password."

"It doesn't matter. How could you?" Mrs. Idacky asked with an incredulous look. "I'm so disappointed in you. Ugh! Don't let it happen again." That was it. She fired off the last shot. I was too soft spoken to put her in her place. She had twice as much teaching experience to back up her accusation. She caught me off guard with the element of surprise. I was too speechless to tell her that her conflict resolution tactics were unprofessional. She treated me like a student with her teacher voice.

I wished I had also said to her, "I am willing to bet you scavenged this activity from another teacher. Authorship my ass; your name isn't even on the document. If you truly wrote this lesson, I seriously doubt you paid a copyright lawyer $300 to have it registered in the Library of Congress. Even if you had, take one hard look at the title of my version of your alleged work. It is different than yours. That is all the legal protection I need from your pathetic possessive soul, because the copyright of my version of that shared activity solely belongs to me, honey. The difference between us is that when I offer to share my lessons with underlings someday, I won't turn around and accuse them of stealing them."

To Hell with Greg Vinoli's Mom

Greg Vinoli was the first student to get caught cheating in my class. Following up on the disciplinary paper work, I contacted Greg's mom at work. I will never forget that phone call.

"Mrs. Vinoli. I am sorry to bother you but your son, Greg, was caught manually overriding the scores of his assignments in my open grade book. He will receive zeros for the assignments he hedged along with a detention for his actions."

"What were you thinking leaving your grade book open for the world to see?" she retorted. "Did you catch him yourself, or did one of his peers rat on him? And where were you this whole time?"

"I errantly left it out in on my front desk, in an area that is restricted to student traffic. At the time this incident occurred, I was in the back of the room, helping a group of students."

"Greg tells me you don't have control of the class and that he's not learning anything in there. Personally, I don't believe you, Mr. whatever your name is. And if Greg was *checking* his grades in the grade book, then it is your fault for leaving it open in the first place. Oh, and one more thing. Don't EVER call me again at work over something this piddley!" Slam. I stood aghast, listening to dial tone.

Bitch! How dare you side with your son over a trained professional, especially pertaining to an incident of this magnitude? Ethics were breached here! I did not sacrifice a good chunk of my lunch hour to take cheap shots from you! That conversation was a wake up call for me to the loser world of deadbeat parents.

Vindication

Lunch periods on paper are duty-free periods if you aren't assigned supervision. Sacrificing a good part of my lunch to call Greg Vinoli's mom was a disaster. If I couldn't make a difference with children who gave up on me in the classroom, there was still hope I could with one of the other 1,900 teenagers in the building whom I didn't have as students.

One day in February, I rounded the corner from the lunchroom area down the science corridor with my hot lunch tray in hand. I couldn't wait to sink my teeth into my dainty hot lunch ration. Down the hall in front of me was a streaker. Not the naked kind, but one who delighted in streaking the floor with the black soles of his shoes. I didn't have to say anything, because I was not officially on hall duty. If a bear poops in the woods and no one is there to report it, did it really happen? I deliberated calling him on it with my tray in hand as he marked up the entire hallway floor in front of me. I knew it would take him a solid ten minutes to scrub the floor clean. I hemmed and hawed over whether to make an issue out of it, until…

"Hey!" I bellowed out. "Get back here." The student turned about and retreated to me. "I believe this mess on the floor is yours? What is your name?"

"Lee."

"Lee who?"

"Lee Simon."

"Alright Lee. Here is what you are going to do. Get a paper towel from that bathroom over there and clean this mess up."

"But I'm going to be late for a club meeting," he pleaded.

"That's your problem. You should have thought about that before you became Picasso."

I stood in that hall ten minutes as predicted while he scrubbed the marks off the floor. I picked at my lukewarm food to help pass time. When he was through, I imparted a send off warning in the event of a second occurrence. Ten minutes of lunch remained. I ambled into the science department office area in search of a microwave for what remained of my now cold food.

My decision to confront a student's immaturity cost me a hot lunch and time off of my feet. It cost me leftover time during lunch I could have used for grading. At least the hallway floor looked clean. I would have made the custodians proud that day.

Dress Code

Even though students pushed the limits with attire that violated the dress code at Caledra Union, I had to insert a true story from my later teaching years in northwestern Wisconsin to kick off this chapter. One workday at the school up there I was milling around the lab stations in the back of my room when I saw Tammi sitting there, wearing a low cut tank top under an unbuttoned flannel shirt, leaning over the table onto her folded arms.

"Tammi, you may want to consider sitting up," I said. Tammi immediately arched her back upright.

"Mr. Parker. Were you looking at my boobs?" she giddily asked, flushed.

"Um, no, Tammi. **THEY...** were looking at **ME**!"

The class fell silent in shock of utter amusement by what I said. They knew what I meant, but it was my professional indiscretion of being blunt that caused me to be summoned again to the chairs of discipline in the high school office-this time at an employment further north.

I actually was summoned a month after the incident, because that was when Tammi objected about how I graded her lab report. She circumvented me and brought the matter directly to the principal, knowing she carried a chip of leverage in her pocket from the boob comment. After clearing up the misunderstanding, I thought the conference was over, when the principal surprised me with the following question.

"By the way, is it true an incident occurred in you class where you commented on her boobs?"

I looked at the administrator incredulously and in a knee jerk reaction said, "Kind of," to verify it. I was suddenly a deer in headlights, a victim of the old bait and switch scam. My mind raced to glean the details of the way I handled Tammi's dress code violation a month earlier. I had a precious few minutes to conjure up details of my encounter with her in a way that would align with her version of the story in a way that would not incriminate me. By this point in time, an administrative secretary had joined us to document me. Every word of my recollected story of that event ventured a step further out onto thin ice. My non-tenured job was on the line. As I rehashed the story, I could see the administrative secretary chuckling in her seat out of the corner of my eye. If this conference marked the end of the road for me, then I would be dismissed on a note of levity and humor. My trials would wind up being the topic of dinner table conversation fodder.

The principal seemed satisfied with my compliant effort to share my testimony before reprimanding me for being so blunt in how I handled the situation. Tammi wore a smile of relief, which befuddled me because I took pride in being approachable in the classroom. Surely Tammi knows males are programmed to be more blunt in the way we communicate. The way I reacted to the situation therefore should not have been deemed a rude personal attack. Nonetheless, it made me wonder how many of my other students had cached cards in their pocket from my in class errors to later use as ammunition against me.

The bottom line is Tammi learned her lesson. She never dressed inappropriately again. Had this been a non-politically correct world, I would have received accolades for how I reprimanded her.

Back to Caledra, in case my job wasn't tough enough my first year, being a male teacher trying to figure out how to deal with classrooms full of girls notorious for pushing the limits of skanky apparel made my job tougher. Depending on the day, I honestly felt damned if I addressed the dress code violation, and damned if I didn't. The fashion trend was a distraction to my job. Skin-bearing midriffs were in, and some girls intentionally wore them to show off pierced belly buttons, tattoos, or the top of their thongs.

The dress code looked good in the student handbook, but it was difficult to enforce. Teachers at Caledra Union weren't consistent in enforcing it, and the same can be said about the staff in every other school I have spent time in. I hated it when students defended their questionable attire by saying, "Well, none of my morning teachers made me change!" A lack of consistent enforcement gives students two wrong messages. First, is the belief that teachers do not care enough about inappropriate attire to consistently address it.

Second, is the notion if a student gets by for most of the day without getting caught, then violating school code is worth the risk. I don't think students consider it a risk if the only penalty is to change clothes. Heck, they are rewarded when they receive undue attention and a free pass out of class to change clothes.

Would you believe Mrs. Rippart, mother of fourth hour student, Samantha, called one day and complained that a classmate of her daughter was a distraction because of what he wore to school on a daily basis? Hello, woman, my job was to teach biology, not to serve as fashion police. I was not the administration whom dealt routinely with disciplining students for violating the student code. It didn't matter, because Samantha's mom was out to target me as the scapegoat for all of her daughter's problems. I countered the wrath of Mrs. Rippart this time after saying, "I wasn't going to infringe on any students' freedom to dress, as long as it was within the allowable parameter of the school code." Did Bill, Samantha's classmate, dress daily in Gothic clothes? Yes. Just because someone dresses up in black doesn't mean s/he glorifies death. I wasn't about to buy into the feigned complaint of intimidation when the perpetrators in black were Samantha's own classmates. In this case, both Samantha and her mom sorely needed to expand their sheltered definition of diversity.

Aside from skanky apparel and the headache Mrs. Rippart gave me in objection to Gothic clothes, the only other dress code violation I wrestled with at Caledra Union was the wearing of jackets in the classroom. Girls violated this policy more than boys because they would get chilly from under-dressing inappropriately in the winter. In other words, they corrected one dress code violation with another. I disdained super padded winter jackets because any movement of the upper torso resulted in a loud chafing noise. High school boys became even more intimidating in size with jackets on. I also did not like to see jackets worn in my classroom because it made students appear as if they were not planning on staying and learn.

Embarrassing Revelations

"This brand new classroom is trashed!" My colleague, Mr. Meatherly barked at me in an unforgiving tone after school one day in fourth quarter. He strolled through the room, noting the vandalism to the lab drawers in the back of the classroom we shared in 1996-1997. Mr. Meatherly taught other sections of biology in the same classroom, periods one through three. Those were the periods I had prep, study hall supervision, and physical science next door. There was no other teacher to blame.

"Look at these walls!" Mr. Meatherly scowled. I was busted. Stop it, Steve! It's not as if *I* vandalized them. Yet, I was responsible for giving students too much down time in class to vandal. I was responsible for not giving them more engaging lesson plans that ran up to the final bell. I was responsible for multi-tasking during class at the expense of surveillance. I was responsible for pissing the students off to the point where they used a permanent marker to etch 'Mr. Parker is a Nazi' above a Swastika on the backside of the beige colored post in the middle of the classroom. I was responsible for allowing my students to tape the Petri plates of their bean seed lab onto the newly painted back wall. I was the one oblivious to the jaw-smacking antics of the spit wad chewers. I was responsible for giving my students too much freedom.

Grayish gooey blotches of spit wads peppered the front wall below the ceiling. Great, now I had a clean up duty heaped onto my schedule after each class-as if I had time for that. I had to conceal the fact that my students were out of control. What happened here stayed here. No wonder my students were giggling today in class. The joke was on me. How did I not catch those little bastards? It doesn't matter now. What mattered was how long this immature fetish of shooting spit wads was going to last.

At first, the spit wad fad was an inconvenience that could be covered up. Then one day, I forgot to check the walls after school and paid the price. The very next day, I spotted a dry spit wad clinging to the wall above the chalkboard. It was rock hard. Since when does an aged spit wad become plaster of Paris? I forged ahead by clambering onto a chair and reached up to pry off the stiff spit wad with a butter knife.

"Ugh!" with a grunt, I dislodged the spit wad, along with a chunk of dry wall.

"Shit! How am I going to cover this up?" I frantically scanned the walls for more. Sure enough, there was a second… and a third… and a fourth, fifth, and sixth one-all at least a day old. I was in hot water for letting this happen and panicked.

How could I resolve this? If I ignored the problem during class, then the students couldn't get a visible rise out of me, and the problem might go away. Telling them how damaging spits wads can be might fuel their appetite for more destruction.

I never did stop the students from shooting spit wads. They ceased doing it one day and moved on to a more horrendous crime - stealing the objective lenses from compound light microscopes. Mr. Meatherly was the first to break the news to me. Mr. Oblivious myself had no clue.

Mr. Meatherly was quick to say that the lenses weren't being stolen during his labs. How was I to argue? Students had no reason to rebel him. Mr. Meatherly's lessons were so structured that his students didn't have time to think about what the lenses would be worth in a Pawn Shop.

I sat down at a lab station in front of one of the compound light microscopes and began working the low power objective lens loose. After a series of six turns, the lens dropped in my palm. I couldn't believe how easy it was to do it obscurely. It could happen in any *supervised* lab. The ease of this vandalism paralleled that of stealing the balls from older computer mice. At the very least, the vandals now had an array of souvenirs from biology.

I learned that once students discover something loose like a lens or a laboratory drawer handle, they continue to toggle it until it comes apart. The same holds true about a keyboard that is missing a couple of keys. In short order, two missing keys becomes four, and then four becomes a discarded keyboard that is missing eight. Think of vandalism to a locker sign. One defamatory remark soon becomes a mural of them. It must be students' inherent nature to exploit a breakdown in the system.

Our next move as a biology department was to sit down and draft a recovery plan. I attended the meeting in shame. We decided to offer a cash reward of an undisclosed amount for their return, coupled with a promise that no disciplinary action or names would be taken. The next morning, a student of mine non-chalantly strolled into our office, asking about the reward. The boy deflected Mr. Meatherly's glare with an "I didn't take them" knee jerk response. Three of the untold number of missing microscope lenses exchanged hands for five dollars out of Mr. Meatherly's wallet that morning.

"Unbelievable," Mr. Meatherly uttered as he stared at the retreating student. I doubted he was the ringleader behind it. The mastermind behind this knew that an undisclosed cash reward from teachers wasn't going to be much. He called our bluff.

My students' heist of the microscope lenses was morally low, but it didn't embarrass me as much as the time when they helped themselves to two of Mr. Meatherly's students' DNA models made with candy. Fortunately, Mr. Meatherly had graded them before they were eaten.

When the thrills of stealing microscope lenses faded, the vandals turned to the jars of preserved animal specimens. Lesson 101 in my diary: if students get too bored while examining the preserved specimens of invertebrates in jars, they will open the lid, dare to sniff the raucous odors that define a biology classroom, and drain the formaldehyde for shits and giggles. The aforementioned actions caused my colleagues to blow another gasket, this time over the inconvenience of having to mix a new batch of preservative solution to restore the partially filled jars to their original level.

Acceptance

I longed for acceptance in all the wrong ways. I wanted to be liked. If a student asked me to buy a fundraiser, I did, even if it meant purchasing a forty-dollar voucher book good for one year within city limits. After hastily purchasing one, I realized most of the participating businesses didn't interest me. The last thing I needed were extra stressors of remembering to carry coupons around with me. I had a hard enough time remembering to use them to get my forty dollars worth back in savings. When one of the restaurants in town wouldn't accept my coupon because it only applied to a certain type of steak platter, I vowed never to buy a coupon book again. The inconvenience of forcing myself to buy things at places I normally would not shop just to save a buck here and there far outweighed the warm fuzzy feelings I had helping out my students in the first place.

Whenever parents, students, or administration criticized me, I longed for positive reinforcement. I became a sucker for flattery under false pretenses. One day in class, Maria approached me out of the blue and said I had the qualities her dad was looking for to be a successful businessman. I didn't need to hear more. I heard what I wanted to hear. Finally, someone disregarded my classroom mistakes and noticed my positive attributes. Before long, I found myself cornered in a three hour meeting with her over-zealous dad, who tried smooth talking me into becoming an Amway salesman. After finally disclosing the true nature of the meeting, I said thanks, but no thanks.

When my science colleagues invited me over to watch a Monday night Packer game, I was there. I wanted to fit in, even if it meant having to tune out the non-stop social bullshit just to watch the game. A sense of belonging had its sacrifices.

When my science colleagues invited me to help build a shelter for abused women, I was there. When the science department promoted participation in the American Cancer Society Memorial Run, I suited up and ran the five-kilometer race. When my colleagues met up for a book review at the local pub, I was there. I did anything for acceptance because I wanted to prove to them I belonged.

Sexual Selection

No teachers I knew took the time to screen visual media of student projects before they were presented. Likewise, I didn't bother to screen my students' visual aids before they were presented on the subtopics of evolution. My students' presentations were supposed to demonstrate mastery of their assigned subtopic on evolution. Instead, the group presentations were dumbed-down and unorganized. Many of the presenters were barely audible. I began to wonder why teachers valued assigning group presentations. Was it for the sake of lesson planning tradition? Was it because the class time allotted for group work made for laid back days and easy lesson planning? Was it a product of constructivist teaching philosophy that emphasized learning is student-centered, not teacher-centered? Do teachers assign in class group projects because they feel students need to develop social skills within the framework of teamwork? My reason for assigning the project was to maintain status quo with the lesson plans of my coworkers.

Nonetheless, I sat through a plethora of uninspiring presentations until Chad and Tony got up to present. Their subtopic of evolution was on sexual selection. They made several posters to illustrate different examples that occur in nature. I was impressed with the quality of the artwork on their posters. Their voices boomed with prideful confidence. Their second to last poster was a robust white tail buck with a huge rack. Their last poster showcased the beauty of male peacock with a fanned out tail. I was just about to congratulate them for a job well done when the tables were turned. They flipped the peacock poster over and on the backside was a cartoon image of a curvy, slender long haired naked woman with supple breasts.

"AND sexual selection occurs in humans too," Chad said.

"Women want to be tan, skinny, and have big breasts," chimed in Tony, "while men strive to become sculpted and muscular."

I was in shock. What was I suppose to say? Where was this in the teacher training? I needed to quickly intervene, but remained speechless. I motioned for a quick transition. What was I supposed to do? Was I to discipline the boys for presenting an undeniable truth to the class? *Homo sapiens* have animal instincts too. Their woman illustration could have been a lot more graphic. I pondered what the harm was in having them surprise the class with a picture of a naked woman, albeit for educational purposes.

The few parents who called in later to protest obviously didn't see it that way. They demanded both boys be disciplined. They fumed at me for allowing this to happen. Come on, like any of this was my fault. Was the last segment of their presentation inappropriate for school? Possibly, but children do a lot of inappropriate things in school that never garner them detentions, like swearing accidentally. I soon questioned if any of the quarrelsome parents had ever let their children play with Barbie dolls. Don't the irate parents have better things to do with their time than to badger me over the phone for a relatively insignificant matter? It was water under the bridge as far as I was concerned. Just because the riled parents may have had a bad day did not give them the right to take it out on me. I was determined not to be their punching bag. Being the new teacher did not make me the scapegoat for everything that went wrong in my classroom.

Later that night I wondered if Chad or Tony had the gall to pull a stunt like that on any of their other teachers. I doubted it. Someday, my students will know not to mess with me. For the time being, it was daily situations like this that caused me to consider myself the worst biology teacher in the state of Wisconsin. If there were a thousand biology teachers in our state, I was certain my rank would have been dead last. How was it possible for me to teach when I exhausted so much energy disciplining kids who took advantage of me? Frank McCourt described in his memoir, *Teacher Man,* how he felt like a fraud in the classroom. I, on the other hand, felt like a failure.

Second Observation

It was another day at the ranch, and I was entrenched in a lesson with my dreaded seventh period biology class. The lesson was on the levels of classification from Kingdom down to species. My wily students easily picked up on the fact this was not my favorite topic, as if they cared about the class in the first place.

Seventh period was my hour of horror with Scott Nachtmare and all of his sidekick fans. Today Scott was his usual self, vociferously commenting about everything off topic in an inappropriate manner. Side bar conversations resonated under my desperate, lecturing voice. My luck ran out when our district principal, Mrs. Stenbaugh, randomly chose this challenging class to observe me for the second time.

There is no such thing as sneaking in if you are an administrator dropping in for an unannounced evaluation. Students have built-in radars for distractions, especially those that come waltzing in. They act different when visitors are in the room. To my chagrin, Scott Nachtmare disrespectfully greeted Mrs. Stenbaugh by asking, "who's that?" the second she entered the classroom. Mrs. Stenbaugh answered Scott's temerity with a quizzical look before giving me an "I can't believe you let your students ask questions like that" look.

I stammered while ascertaining the gravity of the situation. My mind raced as thoughts inundated my head. I knew I was in trouble the moment Mrs. Stenbaugh strolled in. I was caught in the wrong place at the wrong time. My seventh period class was disrespectful on a daily basis, and my lesson that day was uninspiring to say the least. It was a passive lesson plan where students sat in their desks all hour, took notes, and listened to my input. The other two biology teachers, Mr. Meatherly and Mrs. Idacky, had scheduled this day for a lecture on classification, so I went with the flow. Aside from having better behaved classes, my colleague's biggest advantage over me on this particular lesson was they were much more experienced at confidently engaging their students through storytelling and discussion.

Nonetheless, my attention to the lesson was equally as divided as my students'. I couldn't ignore Mrs. Stenbaugh's presence, especially when the bloodbath of written criticism began the minute she sat down. I felt sorry for her pen. If you saw the early 1990's movie *School Ties*, then you may remember to the degree the student McGregor sweat in panic during his French oral final in the presence of his impatient and obstinate professor. McGregor bolted out the door halfway through his exam and plunged into the depths of a nervous breakdown, in light of flunking French class and severing five generations of school ties by not graduating. I felt like McGregor. A beginning teacher without tenure, I could have been fired for no reason at all, let alone teaching boring lessons to a class without effective discipline.

"Well, the show must go on," I said to myself as I continued to give notes off an overhead projector. Keep in mind, this was an era before Power Points became widely used. As I lectured, students who cared copied the notes in the frenzied pace I unveiled them. I periodically asked the students a question to check for their understanding, but the only response I received was the hum of the talkers. The note-takers were too preoccupied trying to keep up with my nervous accelerated note giving pace to field my questions. I have since learned lecturing to students as they take notes is counter-productive. They absorb nothing I say because their attention is on their penmanship, which is something most don't have to begin with in today's computerized society.

If I didn't believe in Murphy's Law, I did after today. Could my day have gotten any worse? I didn't think so, until the light bulb in my overhead projector burned out. My jaw dropped. My fleeting hope for a salvaged lesson vanished in front of my eyes. I toggled the switch to no avail. I didn't know what to do. How could I have? It had never happened to me before. Instead of teaching me practical skill sets like how to troubleshoot such a burned out light on an overhead projector, my professors in college were too busy preparing us how to relate to poverty-stricken students of minority. They even scolded me for calling a certain ethnic group mulattos in front of my classmates one day while at the Work Opportunity Center in Minneapolis.

I since have learned that most overhead projectors have a backup bulb inside of them. All I needed to do was to flip the bottom lever to restore the light source. My future mastery of overhead projector maintenance did not help me on this occasion.

I felt left out to dry this lesson. I had to come out from behind the overhead machine and face the class and my boss. I cradled my hand-held notes in the yellow notepad, which was something that wasn't going to score me any respect points from my audience. I was a recent college graduate with a major in biology. What the heck was I doing falling back on notes? It was because my upper level biology classes were graduate school level, with absolutely no ties to the Wisconsin state standards for tenth grade biology-that's why. I felt overeducated and under prepared to handle the challenges in teaching young adults when I was one myself.

I valiantly tried to win the students' undivided attention the rest of the period, but my chalkboard notes and makeshift demonstrations were a lost cause. My lesson was a failure. With only two classes in which to prepare, there was no reason I couldn't have conjured up a more inspiring lesson. Seventh period biology exposed me as a fraud and failure, and it later showed on my evaluation form. Half of the criteria were check marked as needing improvement.

Mrs. Stenbaugh assigned two teaching specialists to work with me. She naively thought my troubles could be resolved with preventative discipline. She believed I would do a better job at engaging students with more hands-on activities. If students stayed on task, they were less likely to get into trouble. I didn't mind having the opportunity to learn new tactics from teaching specialists. I was just surprised Mrs. Stenbaugh honestly thought teaching specialists could rectify my classroom management issues midway through the year. Was she so far removed as an administrator from her teaching days that she had forgotten the basic principle that once a teacher loses control of a class, he will never get it back?

Team Teaching

As a beginning teacher, you know things are going bad when you are assigned a teaching specialist to come in and work with you a couple days a week. Having the opportunity to collaborate and team teach with a teaching specialist was my last lifeline for improving my classroom management in order to stay full time at Caledra Union. I sadly knew this last ditch intervention was too little, too late.

Sandi introduced herself as the School District of Caledra teaching specialist. She arrogantly and naively believed she was going to transform each of my classes into an idealistic learning center. I questioned her ability to help me as she preached about the dos and don'ts, because all of her tactics specialized in the elementary grade level.

I wondered how her approach was going to work in our team taught lesson. The first lesson involving her assistance was about bacteria and viruses. In it, students were to design a graphic organizer from the presented subject matter.

The day arrived for us to team teach our lesson on microorganisms. Sandi took the brunt of the instructional part, so I could take notes and marvel at her remarkable teaching ability. This is what I observed: Sandi, "blah, blah, blah lesson material, look at me," to student A who wasn't making direct eye contact with her.

"Blah, blah, blah, eyes up here," to student B.

"Blah, blah, blah, I expect your undivided attention," to student C.

You get the picture. Teaching guru Sandi reprimanded students every thirty seconds for not maintaining direct eye contact with her. Even I had difficultly staying focused on the lesson with all of the time spent needlessly demanding their undivided attention. Surprisingly, it was Sandi who disrupted the lesson, not the students. In our post lesson conference, I yearned to ask her why she demanded student eye contact, because I believed student respect was earned, not forced. I reconsidered out of professional courtesy. I was wise enough not to burn bridges with her because I knew she likely would have reported any ill-spirited question back to my boss, Mr. Jonas. He needed no valid reason to fire me, a first year teacher without tenure.

I finished my team teaching experience feeling more hopeless than ever. I couldn't believe that a school district with over three and a half thousand students, grades seven through twelve, had no secondary level teaching specials to effectively assist the upper level teachers.

I initially had a glimmer of hope that a teaching specialist could help me lessen my problems. When that didn't occur, I took on the lone responsibility to become a better teacher. I vowed to never under plan a lesson again. I vowed to research all of the quality hands-on activities I could find for each unit and implement the best ones. I vowed to unleash my fury to design simulations, kits, and games to create learning opportunities no one has ever seen before. I vowed to publish my work and change the way biology is taught today. I sure as hell wasn't going to get crappy evaluations the next thirty years of my life for being content teaching canned curriculum from textbook companies that is boring and anything but user-friendly.

Student Games

After my team teaching experience with Sandi, I brainstormed ways to make students aware of their misconduct. The only idea that came to me was a tactic I observed at a middle school two years earlier. The teacher there wrote names of disruptive students on the board. A second disruptive violation resulted in a checkmark after the guilty student's posted name. A third violation resulted in a second checkmark and a detention. This method was trademark tactic of a system known as assertive discipline.

Why didn't I think of this sooner? This system should please Mr. Jonas because I could monitor misconduct and teach at the same time. If the district thought a teaching specialist limited to elementary level tactics could serve the needs of secondary level teachers like me, then what did I have to lose?

Tomorrow arrived, and I was glowing with a newfound confidence. As lessons progressed, names and checkmarks piled up on the board. The system did nothing to curb the disruptive talkative behavior. Contrary to my high expectations, I couldn't believe my students made a game out of the system. It *encouraged* them to misbehave. They liked the negative attention. Had this tactic been used back when I was in school, I would have been humiliated to have my name written on the board. This generation of students, however, enjoyed being infamous. They knew they outnumbered me and therefore controlled the class.

Fifteen minutes into eighth period, I handed out the first detention to Will with two checkmarks. Then the parade of detentions ensued. Then out of the blue several students belligerently announced they were leaving.

"Where do you think you are going?" I asked.

"To the office," they sniveled.

"You'd rather be in the high school office than here? Why?"

This became a true test of allegiance among the groups of friends. Some left knowing they wouldn't get in trouble due to protection in numbers. How could a majority of the class be wrong about the ineptness of their teacher? Others mustered the courage to leave out of loyalty to their audacious friends. Some of the remaining students were happy as a lark once the obnoxious brats were gone. Maybe now they could learn something. Others just assumed that it would soon become a free period after the exodus.

The latter was right. My mind frantically tried to make sense over why my students were sabotaging my lesson. What could I have done to prevent this? How was it possible for me to continue teaching if my mind was somewhere else?

I couldn't focus on teaching the lesson knowing two-thirds of my class was on their way to the high school office. I cringed at the thought of what the disgruntled students were going to say to the assistant principals behind my back. Who knows how many planned on leaving the school altogether? I could just see the quizzical and irked expression of the hall monitors at first sight of my rebellious students. So much for them getting any grading done in their desks out in the hall this period. I might as well will my problem to them. Imagine the fear that would ripple through the community upon the discovery that unsupervised teenagers were on the loose, ready to cause mayhem! Heaven forbid the trouble teenagers could get into these days. There was a reason the state of Wisconsin adopted a truancy law. It gives the public a peace of mind that children are to be off the streets during school hours.

I carried on with the lesson to take my mind off of the hell I was sure to pay. Sure enough, both assistant principals requested to meet with me immediately after school in Conference Room A. I figured they had so many bones to pick with me that it required both of them to be there. Mr. Jonas opened the meeting with the rhetorical statement, "We need to do something here." No, really? Please don't tell me you sided with the students and all of their creative excuses.

"Who advised you to write students' names on the board as a discipline method?" Mr. Richards, the other assistant principal, asked in utter disbelief. I stared blankly at the table in the conference room as tears welled up in my eyes. At least he didn't insinuate it was my idea.

"I-I…" I stammered, searching for an answer to relieve me from my bourgeoning embarrassment. "I don't know." I conceded with a lie. The less I said, the sooner I could end the embarrassing meeting.

"We advise you not to use that disciplinary practice again. Students who crowded our office said flat out they made a mockery of that system. They *loved* seeing their names on the board. It drew attention upon themselves."

Oh my God. How could I have been so wrong in using that method? What was I thinking? I remember observing that practice effectively used at a middle school, so why was it so terrible for me to implement it? Great, my students are now mocking me out of disrespect. I am a dismissal away from hitting rock bottom of the profession.

Mr. Jonas continued, "We generally don't ever side with students over staff in disciplinary referrals. This matter, however, is unique. We will not be issuing out detentions to the students for talking in your class, because we feel the classroom environment was conducive for talking. On the other hand, every student who visited us eighth period will receive a detention for walking out of your classroom."

The Day a Substitute Came in

The way my classes treated me, I was horrified at the thought of ever having a substitute teacher fill in for me. I did everything in my power to avoid calling in sick, which meant there were a few mornings I showed up to work nauseated. I woke up one morning in February with the flu. I was so achy and listless that I felt like a Mack Truck had run over me, yet I couldn't make the call. No way. I didn't have the energy at six a.m. to phone in detailed lesson plans for a sub. Besides, what comes around goes around. If my students made me sick to begin with, why not return the favor?

OK, I confess. The real reason why I never called in sick was because I didn't want the substitute to deal with my out of control classes. I didn't want him calling me the worst teacher ever in his report. It was a pride thing, because to someone with an expensive college education, why should I have cared about a job with a $24,000 annual salary? I invested a lot of energy covering up my problems. What happened in my classroom stayed there. I didn't want to burden anyone else with my professional shortcomings. I certainly didn't want my parents to know about my failures. They knew something was wrong the times I was eerily quiet during phone conversations. My friends could tell that something was wrong. Non-verbal communication always seemed to unveil my troubles unto others. I couldn't mask my struggles.

It was as if I wore the scarlet letter of shame in the education profession.

One day, I received a memo in my teacher mailbox about an all day mandatory in-service for new teachers the following Wednesday. Surely this had to be a joke. Why would the district schedule a workshop for its new staff members on a school day this late in the year? There was no way I could circumvent needing a sub. Whoever that unfortunate soul was, I feared for his life. My students were going to eat him alive. Forget about my professional development from this untimely in-service – my mind that day was going to be on the survival of my sub.

At the conclusion of the in-service about how to simultaneously meet the needs of students with different learning styles, I raced back to the school to find out how horrible the sub's day went. I wanted to get the bad news over with. Maybe if I got back soon enough, I could apologize to him in person. He was gone by the time I arrived, but fortunately had left me a note on my desk in the science office. I held my breath. This was the moment of truth. I couldn't remember a time where I felt more vulnerable. Surely, the manuscript was about to say, "I will never sub for you again. You are a terrible teacher. Your classes are out of control and your lesson plans are boring. Where did you get certified to teach? Be sure to tell me so I don't send my children there. By the way, I mailed Santa Clause a long list of your students I sent to the office for insubordinate behavior. How do you put up with their crap on a daily basis? Those kids think they own you."

Instead, the brief memo read, "Your students were great and fun to work with. I hope to have the opportunity to sub for you again." I was dumbfounded. I quizzically read the letter again. "How could this be?" I asked myself.

It then dawned on me. Underachieving mischievous students love substitute teachers. In hindsight, students were always happy to see me when I subbed on a regular basis the spring semester the preceding year. They didn't care about my lesser ability to teach the content as a substitute teacher. They simply liked the change - anything but the grumpy, strict teacher.

All this time, I needlessly feared turning over my classes from hell to a substitute. Being absent that day wound up being a three way win situation for the class, the sub, and myself. Why didn't I come to this realization earlier in the year? I would have been obliged to use up my nontransferable sick days, considering I was striving to finish out a one-year contract at Caledra Union. Had my mind been off of my classes during the in-service, maybe I would have learned something.

I went home to crack open a beer. Finally, there was someone in Caledra who wasn't disappointed with my job performance. More importantly, I found a substitute who looked forward to having the opportunity to teach my classes again. I better work on that cough.

Spring Break

Spring break couldn't have come soon enough. It was scheduled as a weeklong break, spanning the last week in April. I needed to get out of Caledra, preferably back to someplace warm like McAllen, Texas, which is where I student taught the fall of 1995. My apartment mate from North Dakota, Troy, still inhabited the place we once co-rented. Troy was a student teacher as well that fall, but now was hired to stay on full time as an English teacher.

There were two things Troy endeared: country musician singer George Straight and Terry LaBonte of NASCAR. The fall of 1995, I learned never to mistakenly use his George Straight shampoo. I also learned never to tip off the winner of a NASCAR race I recorded for him. Troy was as genuine American as they come. He loved his beer, his Mexican-American dates, his auto racing, and his country music. He also helped acquaint me with classic country music. On a typical late afternoon, he would bask in the Gulf Coast breeze with his cowboy boots propped up on the round table out on the balcony, listening to either a classic song from George Straight or Merle Haggard. Beer in hand, he'd say to me, "This is some good shit!"

Well, when Troy got wind I planned a return visit over our spring break, he made sure to treat us with red carpet treatment upon arrival. His place was ours. To whom was I referring? The answer was Devin and Melissa, college buddies who majored in biology with me. Devin and I vacationed near Copper Mountain Ski Resort the previous winter break, where he gave me free downhill ski lessons. He made sure I could snowplow and gracefully take a fall before hopping on a ski lift. I am alive today because of his lessons. Nobody told me the blue diamond runs were equivalent to black diamond runs back in Wisconsin until after I veered off course and crossed over from a green run to a blue one. Not being able to make sharp turns on the precipitous slope, I skidded down the blue slope on my ass while everyone, young and old, zipped past me on skis and snowboards.

I got along with both Devin and Melissa; they, however, didn't. Devin pleaded for me not to invite her. He knew she would misconstrue the invitation as friends to being that of a weeklong date. Devin did not want to feel like a third wheel for the duration of the trip. He knew Melissa better than I did, having gone to the same high school together in Minneapolis. Being the event coordinator, I disregarded his advice and decided to invite both of them. In hindsight, this was another example of a mistake I made because I didn't listen. The 1996-1997 school year was riddled with mistakes I made from not listening and adhering to the sagacious advice of assistant principals, mentors, college professors, or in this case that of a good friend.

Melissa made it pretty clear the second night out on the town on the trip that she had no interest in mingling with the crowd at the bar to find a "hottie." She refused to leave our table and abort her attempts to get to know me better. Things didn't improve the following day in a small border town in Mexico five miles from McAllen, when the bartender messed up and gave her a Pina Colada instead of a Strawberry Daiquiri. He politely took her drink back up to the counter lined with five half full mixers, each a different frozen drink, and dumped it back into the one with Pina Colada (to be used for other patrons). Melissa lost her appetite in more ways than one.

The hair that broke the camels' back was our visit to the nature preserve. Beautiful native birds of the Gulf of Mexico awaited us. Exotic to us, these birds were the ones I dreamed of seeing due to their southern range. To me, this was a once in a lifetime opportunity because the nature preserve was only open to the public one day a week. Despite Devin's interest in seeing the rare birds, he was chomping at the bit to leave the preserve and continue on to South Padre Island, which was the last overnight destination of our trip. In his mind, the longer we stayed at the nature preserve, the less time we had to soak up sun and fun at South Padre. By this juncture of the trip, Devin couldn't stand the thought of being trapped next to Melissa on a floating boardwalk. I felt so rushed on the free nature excursion that I never took time to record the names of the birds. I know I saw a Scissor Tail Flycatcher, a Purple Gallinue, and an Altamira Oriole. There were dozens more birds I saw that I could have added to my life list of seeing, but officially couldn't without documentation. I was so mad at Devin for his rude impatience. I was mad at Melissa for her strong willed disdain towards Devin, and her curtness to me. I was mad at myself

118

for forcing the issue and inviting her to join us on the trip. I was embarrassed to have put up with their petulance towards each other in front of the tour guide.

By late morning, we found ourselves heading down US Highways 77/83 towards the Padre Island Causeway. South Padre was exactly how I remembered it from the previous fall. Spring and fall were semi-tropical. We missed the spring break rush, which was fine with me. The beaches awaited us.

A day and a half later, the dreaded alarm sounded at 4:00 am. We had a forty-five minute drive west on US Highway 100 towards the airport in Harlingen, TX, to catch a first of a connecting flight. Cruising through Los Fresnos at 4:30 am, I had a premonition of bad things to come in this ghost town. It was too quiet. We couldn't have been the only party out and about at this hour of the morning. Sure enough, lights of a squad car lit up the night ahead on the right shoulder. My glance downward at the speedometer was reactionary as I eased up on the gas pedal. Melissa was asleep in the back seat, although I think she checked out three days prior. Devin rode shotgun and arose with the sudden shift of speed.

"Let me handle this," I assured. I had talked my way out of my last four traffic stops for speeding.

"License, please," The county officer snarled. It wasn't the greeting I was hoping for.

"Is this your vehicle?" he inquired after noting the Texas plates and my Wisconsin driver's license.

I had no choice but to confess it was a rental car. He had to ask that question too. Yup, we are tourists – the folks who will not be around in a month to contest a stupid speeding citation in local court-so much for our cover.

"Why were you going that fast?" the officer asked.

"We're behind schedule and need to be at Rio Grande Valley International Airport in a half hour," Devin blurted.

"You'll make it there in plenty of time," countered the officer, as he walked away to fill out the citation.

"Damn it!" I snapped at Devin. "Never say you are speeding because you are running late! Cops never fall for it because they have no sympathy for poor time management! Great!"

Five minutes later, the officer returned with my Wisconsin driver's license and a hardcopy of a $95.00 fine.

"I'll help pay it," Devin offered. "I should have gotten up earlier.

"Thanks, but you weren't the one speeding," I sighed.

Upon arrival at the airport, we received word that our first flight was overbooked. We had all day to return to Minneapolis, so we gave up our seats and accepted a completely different flight plan. In return, Continental Airlines drove us via limousine down to the airport in Brownsville as perk number one. We then flew from Brownsville to Houston and had a four-hour layover, which was not part of our original itinerary. To kill time, we each burned up the twenty-dollar meal vouchers for lunch as perk number two. Continental then flew us first class from Houston to Minneapolis as perk number three. A glass of effervescent Champaign at thirty three thousand feet was enough to make my head spin. For once, I actually had enough legroom to enjoy the spirits. We pocketed perk number four for giving up our seats on our original flight plan, which was a two hundred dollar voucher on any domestic Continental flight, valid for one year from the inscribed date.

Our flight back to the cold reality of my job hit turbulence from a cold, late spring blizzard. Our rocky descent took us into an abyss of white driven snow. I still had a six-hour drive back home, not factoring in the inclement conditions. I mulled over my options and opted to stay the night in Minneapolis with Devin. My executive decision prolonged my spring break another day. Caledra School District penalized teachers who extended breaks by deducting the lost day of contractual instruction from their payroll. Oh, well. I already paid one fine today via credit card. Why would I let a second one phase me? After leaving a message on the phone of a district secretary requesting a need for a sub, Devin and I hit the pubs in uptown

Minneapolis. My lesson plans were not finished, let alone submitted. The substitute was going to have to punt the ball. When I returned Tuesday morning, I discovered the sub didn't bother to even leave a note on my desk as to how the previous day went. That was cold. I tried not to consider the reasons why.

Demotion

Fast–forward the clock to the last week of school. I was standing in the checkout line at Shopko in Caledra and whispered a sigh of resignation, "That's it. I quit. The stress and long hours aren't worth it. I will die of a heart attack by the age of fifty. I failed as a teacher, and I'm walking away from the profession."

I reassured myself that I was not quitting; rather, I was moving on to bigger and better things. Isn't that what sensible professionals do that use teaching as a stepping-stone for better paying careers? Hey, many participants of the Teach For America program do it. As college graduates, they sign up to teach as a starter job without needing full licensure. The caveat is they are placed in hard to staff inner city schools. I vowed throughout the year not to have uncertified Teach For America teachers outlast me in the profession. Well, it was about to happen.

The game was over. My students got the best of me. I should have taken the hint and conceded my failure months back when I was summoned over to the district administrator's office, which is the death knell for a non-tenured teacher. The administrator convinced me to remove Scott from my seventh period class and to let a colleague take over my eighth period class, which was a class I had lost control of back during the first week of school.

To this day, I remembered my last day with that eighth period class. Students verbally contested grading discrepancies of a bacterial lab. I explained to them I may have made some errors out of haste. They didn't seem to care. They were through giving me chances; they were looking for a reason to give up on me. When Devon stood up and said, "This is stupid. I am going to sit out in the hall," I knew all hope was lost with his protest. Devon was my lone supporter in that class for a long time up until then. When I lost him and his passion to learn, the flickering flame of education in that eighth period class smoldered out. Others followed him out into the hall. There were too many to send to the office this time, not that it had stopped me from sending half the class there on previous occasions. I stood in my classroom figuratively alone. I considered continuing on with the lesson; maybe the girls who stayed might be interested in the lesson I worked so hard to prepare. I then realized they were too engrossed in their gossipy chatter to give a hoot about what I had to teach. It was over, I thought to myself. It was just a matter of time before I got the next round of phone calls from angry parents. I was certain the principal was going to be paying me a visit soon.

This time, I was summoned to the district office to meet with the district administrator. By the time he was through debriefing me, I was choking back the tears that had been welling up for months. He handed me a business card of a psychologist he knew and said, "You might as well see him; your insurance covers it." I failed to effectively discipline my classes from the onset, and I paid the price. Consequentially, teaching was damn near impossible. I took a moment to reminisce again on Mrs. Idacky's observation of my eighth period class back in October, "They (my kids) aren't giving you a chance."

I mistakenly tried to toughen out the year by sweeping my discipline problems under the rug, until I figured out a way to resolve them. I was so stressed out that visible dandruff formed on my face-a condition known as *Seborrhic dermatitis*. The pressure I felt to regain control of my classes was overwhelming. Concerned parents, principals, coworkers, and assigned teaching specialists took their turns venting their frustrations at me. The expectations were suffocating and beyond my ability to reach. I taught most of the year in survival mode. I hope my colleagues learned the value of early intervention because in my situation, the intervention was too little, too late.

In 2003, I attended a regional meeting for veteran staff and administrators about mentoring new teachers. Two superintendents at my table were discussing when their new teachers should meet with their mentors _after_ the first week of school. I looked at them square in the eyes and said, "It may be too late by then. Once new teachers lose control of a class, they will never get it back. If it happens, it will become the longest and hardest nine and a half months of life for them."

I knew, entering the teaching profession, I was not supposed to smile until Christmas. I did. I was not supposed to dress like the students and for some reason I did. I was not supposed to chum with them as their friend, yet I did.

I was supposed to be consistent and fair. I wasn't. My rules and expectations were supposed to make sense. They didn't, and many of the petty policies were not enforceable. I was supposed to over plan and keep the students engaged in the lesson as a preventative, disciplinary measure. I under planned, and to make matters worse, I discovered how difficult it was to teach students that had lost all interest in learning. I was supposed to empower students within allowable parameters, but didn't. I should have immediately notified the parents following their child's misconduct, but didn't. I should have had some students write up and sign behavioral contracts, but didn't.

Instead of establishing control of my classes as I had envisioned, students ran roughshod over me. They made a game of my feeble attempts to discipline unruly behavior. There were too many students simultaneously talking out of turn for me to consistently address them in a timely manner. I did not know the students by their first names when it mattered the most during the small window of opportunity I had at the beginning of the year to earn their respect and trust. They exposed my weaknesses and mistakes. Teaching from an outline didn't help my confidence or theirs in me. Most of the energies I needed to teach were spent disciplining students. I wondered what it was like to have attentive and obedient students, just for one day. In hindsight, the only thing I could imagine more miserable than losing control of a class for nine and a half months is when parents lose indefinite control of their children.

I was way too nice. I didn't have to worry about discipline as a camp counselor the previous two summers in Montana. There, we fellowshipped, shared stories, conducted sing-a-longs, and played games. If campers were unruly, I blamed the accompanying adult advisors. It was a problem they brought with them that left with them. The demographic of the children with whom I worked was different at camp than at Caledra Union. Most of the campers wanted to be there. They paid for their several hundred dollar camp sessions with fundraisers. My style of youth interaction in Montana didn't work in Caledra. I failed to understand the difference in demographics and adapt my teaching style accordingly. I banked on having too much fun teaching by visibly being nice and later paid the ultimate price.

Counselor's Office

Mr. Beltez, the shrink, "Enter. You must be Steve."

"Yes."

Yeah, I am the one in despair. Your friend over in the district office referred me to you. Get ready to hear about hell, because I am living it as a teacher.

Mr. Beltez, "Please have a seat. I see you grew up in central Wisconsin."

Seriously, sir, I was just demoted. You have no idea how embarrassed I am to be here. I am not your typical nutcase. You obviously don't know me because I seriously dislike small talk, especially with whom I will likely never see again in my life.

Mr. Beltez, "Please tell me what do you do for a living."

"I teach at Caledra Union High School."

I entered the profession thinking I was a teacher with a knack for inspiring students to learn. In reality, I am an overpaid babysitter because my students have lost interest in learning from me.

Shrink, "What brings you here today?"

"I made mistakes as a beginning teacher and am now paying the price. My classes are out of control. My job has become a nightmare, which stresses me out twenty four-seven. I learned it is impossible to teach if you don't have people management skills."

You, on the other hand, have it made. You get to work with clients in a one on one basis in a private, comfortable setting. This office is a tranquil refuge for helping traumatized people like me.

I could envision myself sitting in that cushioned leather chair behind the desk, counseling clients on a case-by-case basis. Ask questions, listen and then offer advice to get your clients back on their feet. If, however, becoming a shrink required a degree in philosophy, I was in trouble. My philosophy professor at college downgraded me on a paper because I was in her exact words "too analytical of a thinker." I was bothered by her criticism, but I didn't lose sleep over it because as a scientist, I am supposed to be analytical and objective.

Mr. Beltez, "So tell me about your troubles in the classroom."

I stammered out an answer, but what I should have said in retrospect was, "Read my memoir in about fifteen years and then we'll talk. In the meantime, how is it possible for me to teach when my students gave up on me the first week of school? Without classroom control, forget about teaching."

Mr. Beltez, "Who do you blame for your professional troubles?"

"I blame myself. I made way too many mistakes at the beginning of the year. I eventually corrected many of them by the end of first semester, but by then, it was too little, too late. Even my attire was unprofessional some days. When my uncle learned that the holy blue jeans I wore during our family reunion was the same pair I occasionally wore in the classroom on dress down Fridays, his response was, 'No wonder the kids didn't respect you!' I guess that sums it up in a nutshell."

"To a lesser degree, I blame my students and their parents for a lack of support. I blame the antiquated collegiate system in how they train educators. I blame public school districts for not having mentoring guidelines, timelines, and provided conference time allowed for new teachers to meet with their mentors. I blame public school districts that errantly assign elementary teaching specialists to help secondary level teachers. There is a world of difference between teaching tactics that work for pre- versus post-pubescent children. The fact I student taught without a cooperating teacher in Texas for two and a half months while she served on jury duty for a drawn out child custody case didn't help either. Again, all of the aforementioned reasons for my failures are secondary to the mistakes I made."

Mr. Beltez, "Do you feel you have rapport with your students, despite them being disrespectful to your authority?"

"No. Most of them just care about the gossip rings transpiring in my class while I am trying to teach. I thought playing their music during class work time would help me gain rapport, but it backfired. Instead of promoting an environment conducive to learning, the raucous music was more of a detractor. Besides, I was lying to myself by pretending to like half of the music I played. I was desperate to win back their appeal, when I should have been focused on trying to earn back their respect, that is, if they had any for me in the first place."

"I thought attending their extra-curricular events would help earn back their respect. I wanted to demonstrate to them I cared about their achievements outside my classroom. It made no difference. My presence at the volleyball sprawl tournament, the JV baseball game, and at the synchronized swimming performance did nothing to improve my rapport with the participating students."

Mr. Beltez, "How did you manage to survive your classes up to this point in the school year?"

"For starters, playing basketball in the mornings before school with other teachers energized me. I played despite having had two ACL (Anterior Cruciate Ligament) surgeries, one on each knee, both stemming from basketball injuries. I was known as Robocop on the court with my matching set of bulky, metallic knee braces. I then coached freshman girls' basketball after school for most of second and third quarter. My day generally finished on a good note. I guess one could say that bookend basketball was my saving grace."

Mr. Beltez, "How did discipline go as a coach?"

"I had a fresh start with girls a grade younger than whom I taught. My players did not witness my horrors in the classroom."

Mr. Beltez, "What was your motivating factor in your troublesome classes to stick it out until the end of the school year?"

"For the majority of the school year, each class had a core of students who remained attentive, notwithstanding all of the rude talking among their peers," I exclaimed. "I focused on teaching over the talkers in order to reach out to the few who still cared. They were my inspiration. I felt sorry for them for having to put up with all of the noise pollution and time I wasted in class disciplining their immature peers."

"The other motivating factor was knowing that my colleagues were able to successfully handle adversity, in the rare occurrence they encountered it. For example, I doubt there is an undergraduate institution that advises prospective teachers to require their future students to use pencil, not pen, when writing on clipboards for outdoor fieldtrips in the northern states. Why? Because the pens of students froze up during one of the three days our biology department at Caledra Union had taken our students out on an all day field trip to the Kettle Moraine State Forest *in May*!"

Mr. Beltez, "In your opinion, what did you do to make it through the school year to regain your sanity?"

"I handed over the reigns of my eighth hour class to a colleague. In return, I took over his supervisory duty in study hall. Off the record, the district should have cut me back to half time by finding other biology teachers to take over my fifth and seventh period classes as well. I didn't suggest that to the district administrator because I couldn't afford the pay cut. Besides, if I stay in the teaching profession, giving up three classes versus one would have been a resume killer. I also had too much pride. I am determined to ride out the year. By finishing the school day as a study hall supervisor, my day ends on a good note, with exception of the day Mr. Richards, the assistant principal, showed up unexpectedly with a student, caught roaming the hallways with a pass forged with my name. The violator probably targeted me because everyone knows new teachers write out too many passes."

"As for the sanity, I am not sure how to regain it when I am not teaching. It's not like I can free my mind of the misery when the final bell of the school day sounds at 3:30 p.m. I run into students everywhere I go - the mall, restaurants, movie theaters, and even church. Grading never ends. I am also programmed to continuously say, 'I could use that experience, video segment, etc. in the classroom.' "

"I have a history of priding myself in being better at things than in what I really am. I have always been a dreamer. Take fishing for example. I assumed I was a good fisherman just because I spend a lot of time fishing, when in reality I belong to the ninety percent group of fishermen who only catch ten percent of the fish. I also assumed I was a good basketball player just because it was the only indoor sport I competed in. In reality, I am a finesse player who participates in a rugged sport with little ball handling skills. Similarly, I assumed that just because I completed a collegiate teaching degree, I was prepared to effectively teach anywhere in the United States."

"I was over confidant leaving college. My lessons taught in front of my instructors and classmates went well only because I had hours to prepare for each one. I fortunately only have two different preps (classes) in which to prepare each day. I have friends in rural school districts who teach six different classes a day. Imagine the overwhelming sensation they endured transitioning from having to prepare one lesson a week in college educator training to thirty-six a week!"

"I felt on top of my game leaving college. My former students both liked me as a substitute teacher and as a student teacher. My professors and classmates liked me as well."

"No future student of mine could have been as bad ass as me. In our mock teaching modules in college, I sabotaged my classmates' lessons. No one will ever forget Cory Ditmer's lesson on the Middle Ages. As a mock student, I candidly walked over to sharpen my pencil about five minutes into the lesson, and then asked Cory, 'Is it true the early medieval period is called the Dark Ages?' The second he answered yes I switched off the lights, turning the room without windows pitch black. Everyone else was aghast. The fun I had during teacher training blinded me to the seriousness of the job to come at Caledra Union."

Mr. Beltez, "Do you consider the problems you experienced in the classroom situational and mainly limited to your first year of teaching?"

"That depends on the demographics of my future classes, if I stay in the profession," I answered. "Can't you see the blistering dandruff on my cheeks? I am scarred from the stresses of my job. I often dream of what it would be like to teach classes of students with a desire to learn, who are not hell bent on wreaking havoc."

Mr. Beltez, "Besides having cooperative classes, what else do you long for?"

"Positive affirmation. I long to have someone- a superior, a parent, a student – anyone qualified to make a professional assessment of me, say to me that I'm doing a good job. Would you believe I was almost suckered into being a pawn of a students' parent in a money pyramid scheme all because the dad used flattery to allure me with a false sense of worth?"

Mr. Beltez, "In conclusion, it seems to me that you have spent much time introspectively assessing the mistakes you made. My hunch is that if you were to start over next year, you have the ability to earn and keep the students' respect."

"I definitely will manage the classroom differently from the get go. I waited too long to address my classroom control issues and once I did, I was too inconsistent in enforcing the changes. For example, I had zero tolerance on student chatter one day, but not the next – possibly out of sheer exhaustion from sparring with those students who felt entitled to talk freely in my classroom. Please keep in mind that certain lessons demanded my undivided attention because I was less rehearsed in teaching them. The days I cradled my lecture notes were the days I could not multi-task and discipline the way I should have."

"I learned as a teacher your students are impressionable and you aren't going to fool them. If you aren't well rehearsed and/or knowledgeable in a content area, they will know it. They will know the moment you aren't consistent with your values and with how you discipline. The moment a student blurts out something that's inappropriate, all eyes will be on you to see how you handle it – not later, but now. Students will test you before you earn their respect. If you don't earn their respect, enough of them will sabotage your lessons and destroy you. In the end, you will have realized that your dreams of inspiring students to learn will be shattered."

Someday, Frank McCourt will write a best selling memoir, *Teacher Man*, therein describing how teaching forced him to forget his troubles. For me, teaching *was the source of my troubles*.

136

Mr. Beltez, "I believe this concludes our session. I think you have a great perspective on your troubles, and I am confident you will have better teaching experiences in years to come. If you would like to schedule another appointment, stop at the front desk to do so on your way out." That was the last time I saw him.

The Last Day

My remaining days at Caledra Union were numbered. When the final day arrived, it was a bittersweet feeling. I made it. I survived my adjusted goal of sticking it out to the end of the school year. There was no celebration at the end of my solemn ride home. I took time to soak up the cascading rays of sun, leaving the building from work for the last time. They seemed brighter and felt warmer as I ushered myself from the confines of my nightmare. Birds serenaded each other and me. Children were at play off in the distance across the road. I shuttered a deep sigh of relief. My left hand was still squeezing the life out of my summer lump sum check. I paused to look down at the crumpled note. Was it worth my prolonged misery? Yes, it was in the name of dignity, responsibility, and pride. A huge burden was lifting off me as I left the premises in my Chevy Tahoe, because I said goodbye to both Caledra Union High School and to the profession of teaching.

Aftermath of Caledra

I wasn't sure where the road from Caledra was going to take me career wise. I enrolled at the University of Wisconsin, River Falls, the fall of 1997 to take prerequisite courses for veterinary school, which was my new career interest. My daily routine of healing included a mid morning pit stop at the coffee house on campus. The reason for my visit wasn't to warm my soul with coffee. I enjoyed the smell of fresh brewed coffee, but I just hadn't acquired the taste yet. The reason was to sink back into a lounge chair and delve into the news and editorials of a *USA Today*. I didn't have time to enjoy the news the year before or the contemporary alternative music that played in the lounge. I soaked up the guilty pleasures of life between eight and nine a.m. at the coffee house knowing I was no longer teaching a first period class anywhere, risking hell break lose.

I also preoccupied my time studying for the Graduate Record Exam (GRE). In doing so, I came to the frightening realization that my vocabulary was horrible. For years it had impaired my ability to write, speak, listen, and read. No wonder I had a difficult time writing papers. No wonder I lacked confidence speaking. No wonder my reading and listening comprehension were minimal. It all pointed back to my limited vocabulary! I couldn't adequately express myself! How many times over the years did I misconstrue the written or verbal directions of a test question because I assumed an incorrect meaning of a word? I no longer was going to skip over a sophisticated word while reading. I looked up and recorded the meaning of each one in every newspaper and novel I read. I formed piles of cut up note cards with vocabulary words on one side and the definition on the other.

After a yearlong hiatus, I broke my vow and returned to the profession. I was determined never to lose control of a class again. It took a lot of soul searching and gall to step foot back into a classroom. My first year of teaching left me scarred for life. It was not anyone else's fault at Caledra Union but mine. I had to have faith that the changes I made to no avail second semester at Caledra Union were going to make a difference the second time around.

I used the hiatus also to journal my teaching experiences in Caledra as part of my healing process. Most teachers don't have time to journal their professional odyssey, let alone publish it. Aspirations teachers initially have to journal usually dissipate by the end of the workday. Curriculum development and out of class tutoring are just a few of the daily tasks that cause teachers to put journaling on the backburner. Then there are the little things that cause teachers to turn off their back burner, such as: calling parents; I.E.P. meetings; staff meetings; following up on students who arrived to class late without a pass from taking a math test; making a correction to a typo in the header of a handout, printing it off, digging up the old file of it and replacing it; calling a supply company to place an order of a live specimen on hold for an upcoming lab; grading; entering grades;

updating the day's agenda on the whiteboard for all of the classes; and doing inventory.

I am indebted to my mother for resurrecting all of the teaching files I threw away-at the time unbeknownst to me. Mothers know best. She knew I likely was going to stage a return to the profession, and I did.

Facing the Ghosts of the Past

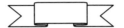

Return to Caledra Union

I drove east on Montgomery Boulevard down the path of my former cross-town commute until the fortress of horrors appeared on the horizon. "I can do this." The earthy smell of spring was in the air. The timing of my return coincided with the 1999 spring break from my new school in northwestern Wisconsin. In contrast to Caledra Union High School, the average annual graduating class size at my new school was fifty-five.

A yearlong sabbatical from teaching was what I needed to lick my wounds, reflect on my teaching practices, and gain enough confidence to step foot in a classroom again. Discipline-wise, I made sure the classes at my new school were manageable to the point I could at least teach from the onset. I was still far from perfect and had a long ways to go on being consistent in handling disciplinary issues. My two other Achilles' heels my second year as a teacher were battling nerves, and getting my curriculum written before my lesson plans were due.

Caledra Union was in session today. Since my departure, Mr. Jonas was promoted to head principal. I'm sure he delegated underlings to handle the discipline problems of the new Mr. Parkers there. He was expecting to see me.

Upon arrival, I entered the building at my own risk. The sophomore students that gave me hell two years ago were now seniors. There were a few who supported me through the hard times I hoped to see, which is the underlying reason why I couldn't let more than two years pass before making a return visit. The hall monitor smiled at me as I made my way to the high school office.

The office ladies didn't remember me. Two years removed, and I was a stranger in the high school office. I guess there were too many people at this school to keep track of.

Mr. Jonas emerged and ushered me into his new office. "Welcome back." We exchanged pleasantries before I updated him about my return to teaching. He knew I was a diamond in the rough two years ago, and he was happy to hear I gave teaching a second chance. He probably felt he spent too much time mentoring me to let it go to waste. There was an exodus of administrators since I left, including Mr. Richards, the other assistant principal who also worked extensively with me. Mr. Jonas was the colleague I longed to see the most. No one, including the biology teachers assigned to me as mentors that school year, knew more about my disciplinary struggles than him. I left his office with a wry smile knowing some secrets are just taken to the grave.

My return visit was already worthwhile when a former student, Nathan, greeted me in the hallway. I was amazed at how much time had passed. I couldn't believe Nathan was going to graduate in a few months. It seemed like yesterday I was his biology teacher. I thanked him again for his unwavering support and for the globe piggy bank he gave me two years ago at Christmas. To this day, that piggy bank is the only one I use as it adorns my dresser. Sometimes it's the little things in life you cherish the most. As we conversed, I wistfully wished more of my former students could have been like him. I was disappointed to hear that he didn't take any more science electives after fulfilling the biology requirement with me. He said he came into biology with a different career in mind. I was relieved to hear I didn't turn him off to the sciences. I was certain that many of his peers were though, because of me. His hurried look at the clock twenty minutes later marked the end of our visit. After departing, I snuck into Room 122 next door. This was the classroom where all hell broke loose two years prior.

Room 122 was quiet as echoes of ghosts past circulated in my head. The two year-old walls were repainted, as was the pillar in the center of the room. No longer did it read, "Mr. Parker is a Nazi" with a Swastika insignia. The top lab drawers that had been vandalized in the back looked halfway decent. Maybe when I left, the spell lifted, and the slums of my inexperience magically reverted back to the newness before I came. My eyes reverted over to the sink where Scott Nachtmare insisted on whacking dry his sopping wet shoes before our confrontation. If I could turn back time, how much of this would have happened had I had a year of experience entering Caledra Union? Why did only the bad memories plague my mind?

The warning bell sounded as students began to trickle into the classroom. Amidst the herd of entering students was another one of my former students, Julia, now a senior. Her eyes immediately locked in on mine. "Oh, my God," she gasped, stopping dead in her tracks, cupping her mouth with both hands. She blushed in shock. She retreated back into the hallway with her friend out of sheer embarrassment over her role in what transpired two years ago. She knew it, and this was a moment of retribution for which I longed. After gathering herself, she tentatively reentered the classroom. "Mr. Parker," she acknowledged, never looking up. In hindsight, if I had given her the chance to coauthor my book, it would have changed the genre from memoir to horror with the inclusion of the details of what truly transpired.

It was time for me to go. I left Caledra the first time in despair. This time I left emotional after two years of healing. For me, it was a once in a lifetime opportunity for catharsis. Tesla's melancholy power ballad *Paradise* resonated through my speakers as I tearfully drove down memory lane and out of town.

Epilogue

Hopefully you enjoyed my story and became edified in some of the struggles new teachers face. Whenever a teacher loses control of a class, or in my case, classes, there is no Hollywood ending to the story. The silver lining of my cloud is my experiences helped me become a better teacher and person. The important thing is you care enough about public education to have taken the time to read this book for hopefully a better tomorrow.

Literature Cited

[1] Maraniss, D. (1999) When pride still mattered. A Touchstone Book (back cover)

[2] Maraniss, D. (1999) When pride still mattered. A Touchstone Book (161, 213)

[3]Ibid.

About the Author

Steven Parker lives in Cornell, Wisconsin, with his wife, Karen, and two children. He teaches biology, advanced biology, and field ecology in northwestern Wisconsin. When he is not working or spending time with family, he enjoys fishing, bow hunting, photography, writing, and nature hikes.

Steven has published educational products through five different corporations. He was one of the first 25 teachers in North America to become a 5 Product Developer through Science Kit & Boreal Laboratories (NY). The following page shows a list of his publications.

~Publications~

Flinn Scientific (IL)
Mystery Slide Microscope Kit

Lab Aids, Inc. (NY).
Molecules of Metabolism Kit

Teacher's Discovery (MI)
For Life Science Teachers: 112 Activities and
Tactics

Science Kit & Boreal Laboratories (NY)
Salmon Run
Migration Game
Natural Selection: A Game of Chance
Bones No Bones Fun Pack Kit
Symbiosis Posters

Front and back cover photos of the office by Steven
Parker
Outdoor photo of the author by Karen Parker
Indoor photo of the author by Steven Simon

Author/editor note: All names of people, schools,
and towns of employment have been changed

To order additional copies of *Chairs of Discipline*,
please contact:

Publishers ExpressPress
200 West 5th Street South
PO Box 123
Ladysmith, WI 54848

715-532-5300
800-255-9929
FAX: 715-532-4888

Order *Chairs of Discipline* online @
www.PublishersExpressPress.com
$16.95

or order on Amazon (www.Amazon.com)
Enter ISBN: 978-1-935920-00-7